PERILOUS TIMES

By the same author

AFTER MIDNIGHT
HEADLINE PULPIT
NAKED TRUTH

DAILY GOSPEL

PERILOUS TIMES

by
PAUL B. SMITH, B.A., D.D.
Minister of The Peoples Church, Toronto

Foreword by
HYMAN J. APPELMAN, A.B., L.L.M., D.D.

MARSHALL, MORGAN & SCOTT
London

MARSHALL, MORGAN AND SCOTT
116 BAKER STREET
LONDON W1M 2BB

AUSTRALIA
119 BURWOOD ROAD
BURWOOD
VICTORIA 3125

NEW ZEALAND
P.O. BOX 29012
GREENWOOD'S CORNER, AUCKLAND

SOUTH AFRICA
33 CENTRAL AVENUE, BOX 17
PINELANDS
CAPE

CANADA
HOME EVANGEL BOOKS LTD
25 HOBSON AVENUE
TORONTO 16
ONTARIO

THE PEOPLES CHURCH, TORONTO
347 SHEPPARD AVE. EAST
WILLOWDALE
ONTARIO

U.S.A.
GOSPEL ADVANCE PRESS
P.O. BOX 339 SALIDA
COLORADO 81201

© Paul B. Smith 1967

First impression 1967
Second impression 1967
Third impression (paperback) 1969
This edition 1974

ISBN 0 551 05377 1

Printed in Great Britain by
Lowe & Brydone (Printers) Ltd, Thetford, Norfolk

FOREWORD

PERILOUS TIMES is long overdue. The tidal waves of liberalism and apostasy sweeping across the earth call for it. No one is better able to write the book than Doctor Paul B. Smith. Young so that he is *en rapport* with the thinking of the often described "rebellious generation"; old enough so that he speaks with accumulated wisdom. This is a Must for all ministers —for that matter, for all Christians, particularly those who have any responsible positions in our churches. The book is not overloaded with technical language, neither does the author allow himself the common clichés so prevalent. The language is chaste, easily understood, furnishing food for thought as well as answers to the questions raised everywhere on the Church and the times.

Doctor Smith's experiences as the Minister of the largest church in Canada, in attendance, in missionary outreach, as well as his Evangelistic Campaigns and Missionary-Prophetic-Bible Conferences literally around the earth, give him the right *and the ability* to speak authoritatively. His treatment of each controversial subject is eminently fair, born out of much prayerful thinking, reading and questioning.

The ten chapters on "How to Study the Bible" will grow into the proportions of a classic on this subject that is so needed today when more Bibles are sold, and probably less Bible reading done, than in years. Modern translations of the Bible in the language of today are good, but here are chapters that will cause the readers to go or go back to the Bible with a new insight of its contents.

Perilous Times should be on the shelves of all preachers, and should be required reading for all Christian College and Seminary students. *Perilous Times* is needed.

Hyman Appelman

Kansas City, Missouri

CONTENTS

		PAGE
	Foreword	5
	Preface	9
I.	Liberals, Evangelicals, and Inspiration	11
II.	The Apostate Church	15
III.	Brainwashed!	25
IV.	The New Sunday School Curriculums	30
V.	The New Morality	59
VI.	The Sin of Sodom	67
VII.	The Bible and Integration	74
VIII.	The Bible —Do I Know the Author?	81
IX.	The Bible —Do I Know the Meaning?	86
X.	The Bible —Do I Know the Application?	91
XI.	The Bible —Do I Know the Prophetic Significance?	94
XII.	The Bible —Do I Know the Context?	98
XIII.	The Bible —Do I Know the Complete Revelation?	102
XIV.	The Bible —Do I Know an Inference from a Fact?	107
XV.	The Bible —Do I Know Who is Speaking?	113
XVI.	The Bible —Do I Know To Whom It Is Speaking?	117
XVII.	The Bible —Do I Know the Experience of Obedience?	123

Dedicated To
REV. DANIEL L. EDMUNDSON, PH.D.
who thought with me through many
of these problems and compiled
the lists of scientists and
theologians in Chapter IV.

PREFACE

FOR many years modernism in Canada has been camouflaged. Many of the people in the pews thought their ministers still held to some form of historic Christianity. In most cases the preachers made little attempt to state what they really believed, content to leave their parishioners quite in the dark. Then in 1964 The United Church of Canada published the first part of its "New" Sunday School Curriculum—a series of books and lessons that had reverted to the old extreme modernism of the last century. Reaction was immediate and stretched from coast to coast, and for the first time in recent years liberal ministers confessed that they were liberal and conservative ministers decided that it was high time to stand up and be counted. The sheep were being separated from the goats and a large number of people found that they were lost somewhere between the two.

The first seven chapters of *Perilous Times* include some of the material I preached from the pulpit and wrote for the newspaper during the years 1964-6. I have attempted throughout to concentrate on the issues rather than the personalities involved. This has not always been an easy line to draw. Some of the attacks of our liberal friends have been vicious and vindictive, and occasionally our conservative position has been set forth with more anger than argument. This I regret.

It is important to remember that it is often necessary to attack a man's position, and sometimes quite violently. However, it is never helpful to anyone to attack the man himself. I have some good friends in modernistic churches and among liberal ministers. I believe they are wrong, anti-Biblical, and Antichrist, and I do not hesitate to say so. However, I would sit down with any one of them over a cup of coffee at any time. They are in the world for which our Lord died and they are part of the parish that is my responsibility. If they are to be won to Christ it is essential that the lines of personal communication be kept open.

The last ten chapters of *Perilous Times* suggest a practical positive approach to the study of God's Word. It is of vital consequence that we accept the Bible as the infallible and authoritative Word of God. This is the thesis of the first part of this book. It is equally important that we become diligent students of the Book we rise to defend. This is the essence of the last part of this volume.

Apostasy that stems from basic doubts about the authenticity of the Divine Library is not a problem that is peculiar to Canada. It has seeped across the world so that today there are few places that have not been contaminated.

P.B.S.

Toronto, Canada
November, 1966

CHAPTER I

LIBERALS, EVANGELICALS, AND INSPIRATION

THE basic difference between a Liberal and an Evangelical concerns the Inspiration of the Bible. When the Liberal is confronted by problems, he concludes that the Bible is wrong. He may try to explain the error in four ways:

(1) The passage involves legend, allegory, folklore, or myth; and if so, as long as the spiritual point is made, the facts do not have to be correct.
(2) The purpose of the Bible is not to record science or history, but religion. Therefore, if the religious intent is right, the science and history can be wrong.
(3) The authors of the books of the Bible lived too long after the events which they recorded to have the authority of eye-witnesses, and, therefore, they were subject to many mistakes. Some of their mistakes are a result of the oral tradition which they claim preceded the actual writing of the Bible by many centuries. Pass a story along by word of mouth and in a very short time the facts are incorrect.
(4) The writer may have been a contemporary but he was ignorant of the facts in this particular case, or chose to alter them to serve his own purpose.

When the Evangelical is confronted with Scriptural problems, he assumes that the Bible is infallible and the error is to be found in himself. He may pinpoint the problem in one of three areas:

(1) He may conclude that his interpretation of the Bible is incorrect and he will change it so that it fits the facts.
(2) He may find the trouble in his translation of the original manuscripts. He knows that we do not have the original writings, but he concludes that if we did, many of the problems he faces would be solved.
(3) He may conclude that the science which seems to contradict the Bible is wrong. In this connection it should be pointed out that the Evangelical does not disregard the great value of modern science and its inestimable contribution to world civilization. However, he is alert to the fact that science is never stationary. What is factual today may be error fifty years from now. For instance, most of our older generation learned that a straight line is the shortest distance between two points. We are told that in modern mathematics and science this just is not true any longer. We also learned that parallel lines never meet. However, the space age has proved that parallel lines do meet. It was science that concluded many centuries ago that the world was flat. Today no scientist would accept this position. Thus, the Evangelical concludes that in some cases where present day science seems to contradict the Bible, future generations may produce new scientific facts in which there is no Scriptural contradiction.

LIBERALS, AND INSPIRATION

The Liberal theologian faces the problems of Scripture with the question, What's wrong with the Bible? The Evangelical theologian faces many of the same problems with the question, What's wrong with me? For the Liberal the Bible is not infallible. For the Evangelical the Bible is always infallible.

Literal and Infallible

Evangelicals do not interpret everything in the Bible literally. We have always recognized the fact that there are many parables and symbols throughout all of the Scriptures. Evangelicals have always accepted the existence of hyperbole in the Word of God. For instance, when Matthew says that all Jerusalem and all Judea went out to hear John the Baptist, we do not believe that the word 'all' here means that every man and woman and boy and girl in the entire area went to hear John. This is a clear case of exaggeration, and all Bible readers have been aware of the fact that this is simply a way of pointing out the size of the crowd that did go out to hear John.

The Evangelical does not contend for a literal interpretation of Scripture, but an infallible one.

Verbal and Plenary

The Evangelical may describe his view of inspiration as Verbal or Plenary, or sometimes a combination of both.

By Verbal Inspiration he means that the original manuscripts were verbally inspired by God. No intelligent Evangelical has ever believed that his particular translation of the Bible is verbally inspired.

By Plenary Inspiration he simply means that the Bible is completely inspired, but this leaves room for the use of the vocabulary of the human author. In this view, God tells the writer exactly *what* to say but he is left to say it in his own words. Plenary Inspiration allows a variety of language but it does not permit factual mistakes.

Many Evangelicals believe that part of the Bible is verbally inspired—that is, directly dictated by God, but that other parts involve Plenary Inspiration—in which the author recorded exactly what God wanted him to say but he said it in his own words.

CHAPTER II

THE APOSTATE CHURCH

BOTH the Old and New Testaments have a great deal to say about false teachers and apostasy in general. There are many passages which warn us that there will be false teachers and tell us what our relationship to them should be. Here are sixteen examples from the New Testament.

Matthew 7: 15, 21–24—"Beware of false prophets, which come to you in sheep's clothing, but inwardly they are ravening wolves. Not every one that saith unto me, Lord, Lord, shall enter into the kingdom of heaven; but he that doeth the will of my Father which is in heaven. Many will say to me in that day, Lord, Lord, have we not prophesied in thy name? and in thy name have cast out devils? and in thy name done wonderful works? And then will I profess unto them, I never knew you: depart from me, ye that work iniquity. Therefore whosoever heareth these sayings of mine, and doeth them, I will liken him unto a wise man, which built his house upon a rock."

These false prophets obviously pass themselves off as true prophets. They hide behind a front that would indicate they are teaching the Word of God, but in reality they are not. Particular emphasis is laid upon "these sayings of mine". The entire illustration of the wise and foolish builders at the end of this chapter is to teach us the importance of obeying the teachings of Jesus Christ. These are to be found in the Bible. We have no other source.

Matthew 15: 8–9—"This people draweth nigh unto me with their mouth, and honoureth me with their lips; but their heart is far from me. But in vain they do worship me, teaching for doctrines the commandments of men."

The people who are under consideration here are not outsiders but those who pose as followers of God. Our Lord's objection to them is that they follow the dictates of their own reason even though the results may constitute a violation of the doctrines of the faith. Certainly we are expected to use our intellects. There is nothing wrong with investigating the things we believe, but always this should be done with the basic assumption that the Bible is right and where there is a conflict we give the benefit of the doubt to the Word of God.

Matthew 24: 11—"And many false prophets shall rise, and shall deceive many."

The emphasis in this verse is to the number of false teachers that we can expect and the number of people whom they will deceive. False teaching will not be carried on by isolated heretics. There will be many of them wielding an influence over large segments of the religious society.

Acts 20: 27–30—"For I have not shunned to declare unto you all the counsel of God. Take heed therefore unto yourselves, and to all the flock, over the which the Holy Ghost hath made you overseers, to feed the church of God, which he hath purchased with his own blood. For I know this, that after my departing shall grievous wolves enter in among you, not sparing the

THE APOSTATE CHURCH

flock. Also of your own selves shall men arise, speaking perverse things, to draw away disciples after them."

The Apostle Paul has just reminded these people that he has taught them everything that they need to know. "I kept back nothing that was profitable unto you." We now know that Paul not only taught the things that we should know but he also committed them to writing so that they would never be forgotten and the Spirit of God has seen to it that they are preserved unto this day.

In this passage Paul warns the people that from among their own ranks teachers would arise who would try to change the doctrine that he had taught and that they would "draw away disciples after them". He labels them "grievous wolves".

Romans 16: 17-18—"Now I beseech you, brethren, mark them which cause divisions and offences contrary to the doctrine which ye have learned; and avoid them. For they that are such serve not our Lord Jesus Christ, but their own belly; and by good works and fair speeches deceive the hearts of the simple."

Once again the Church is warned that false teachers will come, and once again the danger will be that they will try to change the doctrines that he has taught them. These will be men who have the ability to use a fine vocabulary and deliver intelligent discourses. Paul's advice is to "mark them and avoid them".

2 Corinthians 11: 14-15—"And no marvel; for Satan himself is transformed into an angel of light. Therefore it is no great thing if his ministers also be transformed as the ministers of righteousness; whose end shall be according to their works."

The point that is emphasized in these verses is that these false teachers will appear to be legitimate ministers. Perhaps pastors of churches, professors in theological seminaries, or executives of religious organizations. The very crowd whom we would expect to stand for the Bible and uphold it will spend their energy and dissipate their intellect in an attempt to destroy its authority.

Galatians 1: 6-9—"I marvel that ye are so soon removed from him that called you into the grace of Christ unto another gospel: Which is not another; but there be some that trouble you, and would pervert the gospel of Christ. But though we, or an angel from heaven, preach any other gospel unto you than that which we have preached unto you, let him be accursed. As we said before, so say I now again, If any man preach any other gospel unto you than that ye have received, let him be accursed."

The Bible gives us no authority to change the Gospel. It warns us against doing it. The core of the Gospel message is that man must believe in Jesus Christ if he is to be saved and that apart from this, he is lost. The Liberal theologians of our day would like to change the Gospel so that it includes the peoples of the other religions of the world. Those who accept the Gospel are to be rewarded by Heaven and those who reject it are to be condemned to Hell, but now we are asked to believe that no one will really go to Hell, and we cannot be very sure about Heaven except as it may relate to this world. If any man poses as a minister of the Gospel but obviously changes it, the Bible says, "Let him be accursed."

THE APOSTATE CHURCH

1 Timothy 1: 18–20—"This charge I commit unto thee, son Timothy, according to the prophecies which went before on thee, that thou by them mightest war a good warfare; Holding faith, and a good conscience; which some having put away concerning faith have made shipwreck: Of whom is Hymenaeus and Alexander; whom I have delivered unto Satan, that they may learn not to blaspheme."

Timothy is probably being reminded of his ordination vows. Otherwise there is not much significance to the words "according to the prophecies which went before on thee". At that time this young minister had made certain promises before God in the presence of those who laid hands upon him. Paul reminds him of that day and the faith he promised to uphold, and urges him to resist anybody who makes "shipwreck" of the faith. Paul deliberately names the particular men whom he has in mind and states their condemnation.

1 Timothy 4: 16—"Take heed unto thyself, and unto the doctrine; continue in them: for in doing this thou shalt both save thyself, and them that hear thee."

We are not warned against changing our methods of doing things but we are urged that under no conditions should we change the Gospel or the doctrine. The Evangelical churches of the world are famous for using Modernistic methods while they maintain the old-fashioned Gospel. Liberals are equally renowned for adhering to old-fashioned methods but insisting upon changing their beliefs. Most Modernistic churches cling desperately to sixteenth-century music, seventeenth-century robes, and an eighteenth-century order of service, but in the midst of these old-fashioned methods they expound ideas that are difficult, if not impossible, to find in the Bible. In this passage, once again Paul urges Timothy to continue in the same doctrine.

1 Timothy 6: 3–5—"If any man teach otherwise, and consent not to wholesome words, even the words of our Lord Jesus Christ, and to the doctrine which is according to godliness; He is proud, knowing nothing, but doting about questions and strifes of words, whereof cometh envy, strife, railings, evil surmisings, Perverse disputings of men of corrupt minds, and destitute of the truth, supposing that gain is godliness: from such withdraw thyself."

After reiterating that the important things are "the words of our Lord Jesus Christ" and the "doctrine which is according to godliness", Paul adds that one of the characteristics of false teachers is that they will waste a great deal of time on questions which do little more than produce strife, envy, railings, and surmisings. It is a sad day when the Church of Jesus Christ has nothing to offer its people but questions. The Bible is a Book of answers. People will always ask questions but the minister of the Gospel is expected to give some answers.

2 Timothy 3: 1, 5, 7, 14–17—"This know also, that in the last days perilous times shall come . . . . Having a form of godliness, but denying the power thereof: from such turn away . . . . Ever learning, and never able to come to the knowledge of the truth . . . . But continue thou in the things which thou hast learned and hast been assured of, knowing of whom thou hast learned them; And that from a child thou hast known the holy scriptures, which are able to make thee wise unto salvation

THE APOSTATE CHURCH

through faith which is in Christ Jesus. All scripture is given by inspiration of God, and is profitable for doctrine, for reproof, for correction, for instruction in righteousness: That the man of God may be perfect, throughly furnished unto all good works."

We begin our search for the truth when we reach the age of responsibility and that search continues throughout our lives until we find Jesus Christ. We do not stop thinking at this point, but as far as the ultimate questions of life are concerned, the answer is to be found in the Person of the Living Lord. One of the characteristics of false teachers is that they are "ever learning, and never able to come to the knowledge of the truth".

In these verses we are told emphatically what doctrine we are to keep and what teachings should never be changed. They are those that are incorporated in the Holy Scriptures. When we begin to doubt the Scriptures, we join the ranks of the apostates. The command as far as the child of God is concerned is "from such turn away".

Titus 1: 16—2: 1—"They profess that they know God; but in works they deny him, being abominable, and disobedient, and unto every good work reprobate. But speak thou the things which become sound doctrine."

The Bible, and particularly the New Testament, is a Book of dogma despite the efforts of Liberal theologians to state differently. Some modern churches refuse to let their people recite a creed because they do not believe that there are any absolutes—even in doctrine.

The Bible stresses the fact that ministers should preach "the things which become sound doctrine", and that if they do not they are "abominable, and disobedient, and unto every good work reprobate".

Titus 3: 9–11—"But avoid foolish questions, and genealogies, and contentions, and strivings about the law; for they are unprofitable and vain. A man that is an heretick after the first and second admonition reject; Knowing that he that is such is subverted, and sinneth, being condemned of himself."

False prophets usually approach the Word of God with a critical attitude. They look for problems where there are none and ask questions to which there may be no answers. Every Christian should study the Word of God, but it should not be approached with doubt and misgivings but rather with trust and confidence. Beware of teachers who ask questions and then can answer them only by discarding some section of the Bible. We are urged to admonish this kind of person once or twice and then reject him.

2 Peter 2: 1–3—"But there were false prophets also among the people, even as there shall be false teachers among you, who privily shall bring in damnable heresies, even denying the Lord that bought them, and bring upon themselves swift destruction. And many shall follow their pernicious ways; by reason of whom the way of truth shall be evil spoken of. And through covetousness shall they with feigned words make merchandise of you: whose judgment now of a long time lingereth not, and their damnation slumbereth not."

This passage states in direct language that false teachers are damned.

2 John 6–11—"And this is love, that we walk after

THE APOSTATE CHURCH

his commandments. This is the commandment, That as ye have heard from the beginning, ye should walk in it. For many deceivers are entered into the world, who confess not that Jesus Christ is come in the flesh. This is a deceiver and an antichrist. Look to yourselves, that we lose not those things which we have wrought, but that we receive a full reward. Whosoever transgresseth, and abideth not in the doctrine of Christ, hath not God. He that abideth in the doctrine of Christ, he hath both the Father and the Son. If there come any unto you, and bring not this doctrine, receive him not into your house, neither bid him God speed; For he that biddeth him God speed is partaker of his evil deeds."

Love seems to be the theme song of the Modernist and to read his writings or hear him preach, one would think there was no such thing as judgment in the Bible. The inference is that what you believe is not very important as long as you love everybody. In the "new morality" this idea is carried to an extreme that removes all standards of moral conduct and supposes that almost anything is right if the motivation is love.

These verses present an interesting definition of love that ties it inseparably with the commandments that "ye have heard from the beginning". Love is best demonstrated by adhering to the commandments of the Word of God. Anything else is not love but rather the spirit of antichrist.

Jude 3-4—"Beloved, when I gave all diligence to write unto you of the common salvation, it was needful for me to write unto you, and exhort you that ye should earnestly contend for the faith which was once delivered unto the saints. For there are certain men crept in unawares, who were before of old ordained to this condemnation, ungodly men, turning the grace of our God into lasciviousness, and denying the only Lord God, and our Lord Jesus Christ."

It is important not only that we believe sound doctrine and hold fast to the Gospel of Christ, but also that we contend earnestly for the faith. Whenever there is an opportunity, we should be willing to stand up and be counted.

We might sum up these passages as follows: There will be false teachers, they will influence a large number of people, they will come from inside the church, they will seek to change the doctrine and the Gospel, they will be intelligent and gifted speakers, they will approach the things of God with doubt and questions, but they are doomed to condemnation. Our attitude towards them should be: Mark them, avoid them, warn them, withdraw from them, and maintain our own faith in the teachings of Jesus Christ and His apostles as they are found in the Holy Scriptures.

CHAPTER III

BRAINWASHED!

WHEN I was in Russia in 1958 I had three different guides. As they gradually inflicted the "Party Line" on me I observed how thoroughly "brainwashed" they were. They sincerely believed that all the really strong thinkers were either in Communist countries or wished they were and that anyone who did not hold the Communist view had not been exposed to any real good scholarship. Most Communists do not actually hate us, but they do feel desperately sorry for us.

In the theological field this is a fairly accurate description of a liberal. He has been so utterly "brainwashed" that he sincerely believes no really well-educated person could be a Fundamentalist. How could he be, when all the scholars and all the good schools are liberal?

It is hard to believe that men of this calibre are not aware of the interminable list of Conservative theologians who have been waging a war with them for more than a century. Whom do they think they have been having their controversy with—the little man who wasn't there? Where do they think these opponents about whom they have bothered to write millions of words have been trained—in colleges that do not exist?

Could it be possible that they really believe they are the only people who know the ancient languages and something about where and how we got our Bible?

Yes, yes, yes—on each count. Liberal Theologians are perhaps the most completely "brainwashed" group in the world. This is the "Party Line" that has been handed down to them from their universities and seminaries—"scholarship and modernist are synonymous and ignoramus and fundamentalist are synonymous".

And these dear "brainwashed" brethren have never bothered to take off their blinkers and have an honest look on the other side. If they had, they would know that any well-informed Fundamentalist could line their library shelves with books and commentaries written by men just as brilliant as any liberal theologian, cognizant of all the problems in the Bible, conversant with Hebrew and Greek, and very much alert to every modernistic theory and interpretation—but who still hold and write a fundamental theological position.

There is nothing in modern theology that has not been adequately answered in a dozen different ways. If anyone wants to know the answers all he has to do is consult one good conservative commentary. He doesn't have to accept the answer, but at least if he is an honest man he will admit that it is there.

But the liberal prefers to leave questions hanging in the air as if he were the first one who ever thought of them and as if no one has ever been able to answer them. There is very little in The New Curriculums that

BRAINWASHED!

has not been kicked around by theologians for more than a hundred years. Any scholar who has lived within this period has been cognizant of all the major issues in The New Curriculums and every conservative theologian since the middle of the nineteenth century has discussed them and given satisfactory answers—so that any man who really wants to can accept the Bible as infallible and know that he is standing on good scholarly ground.

This is why the Editor of one large denominational magazine can declare so blatantly, "We must change the doctrine of Hell." He suffers from liberal "brainwashing". He must actually believe that all the intelligent people in the world have long since dropped the idea that the Bible is infallible. And his magazine above all else must be intelligent.

Of course, when a man or magazine reaches this point, the sky's the limit. From there you can go anywhere you want. Believe what appeals to you and reject what does not. There is no other criterion for the modernist.

He protests that he accepts those parts of the Bible that are compatible with the spirit of Jesus. But then he proceeds to be the judge of that spirit. How does he know, for instance, that the story of the Good Samaritan represents the proper spirit but the story of the Rich Man and Lazarus does not? Mercy and justice, love and punishment, indignation and compassion are to be found combined throughout the Gospels. Who is man to decide which is the true spirit? And why not accept both as completely compatible in the personality of God and His Son—just as the Bible portrays them.

Certainly, I may not understand how the idea of eternal punishment can be compatible with the idea that God is love. But then there are many things about God which seem incompatible to my little mind.

In our home we have a blue budgie and a white cat. Jesus told us that God is concerned about little birds and sees them when they fall. If this is so, why did the same God make my white cat with an instinct that makes it her greatest ambition to catch the budgie, torture it for a while, and then eat it? To me, it seems quite incompatible that the same God would have created both.

I suppose if I was God I would know the answer to this conundrum and it is probably quite simple. But I am not God and so I do not demand that we obliterate either the budgie or the cat. If these pets were doctrines of the Bible, one of them would be in grave danger if a liberal theologian happened along.

The doctrine of Hell will never be brought into doubt by new discoveries. Archaeological investigations will neither cover nor uncover Hell. Science has no bearing on it. Unless someone comes up with an authentic manuscript that proves the New Testament writers did not quote Jesus accurately on the subject, we will always be confronted with an account that teaches the fact of Hell.

Hell has been a doctrine of the church as long as there has been a church. Apart from an occasional freethinker and a few heretics, scholars in the church have made Hell a part of their creed.

So our belief or rejection of Hell has nothing to do

with our great intellects. Better minds than ours have accepted it as a fact. It is as simple as this: if we accept the Bible, we believe it; if we reject the Bible we may refuse to believe it.

CHAPTER IV

THE NEW SUNDAY SCHOOL CURRICULUMS

THERE has been a rash of "New Curriculums" in many of the liberal denominations throughout North America. Actually, the name is somewhat misleading because there is nothing very modern about them either in theology or method.

The theology is old-fashioned modernism. It was revolutionary and shocking when it seeped like sewage out of Germany during the latter half of the nineteenth century. It consists of a denial of many of the doctrines of historic Christianity, an egotistical fear of the supernatural and a humanistic emphasis on social problems rather than the Gospel.

It was pushed far into the background by Neo-orthodoxy and during the pressure of the World War II years was almost forgotten. Humanism always takes a nose dive when the problems of the world become so intense that men demand answers to the ultimate questions of life. It can prosper only when man thinks he still has a degree of control over his destiny.

The "Big War" is now more than twenty years behind us and the new generation thinks of the Great Depression as something that happened in the "olden days". Despite the grave problems that face our times, man still believes he holds the throttle in his own hand

NEW CURRICULUMS

and can eventually make a soft landing in a sort of Utopia.

In this atmosphere the old "rank modernism" has been revived and has been published in a popularized form in the current curriculums for today's Sunday Schools.

Neither is there anything very revolutionary about the methods of the New Curriculums. Anyone who has been familiar with the evangelical materials that have been used for at least twenty-five years will find little in the much toted courses that he has not seen before.

If you have studied one set of New Curriculum books, you have studied them all. There is very little difference since they are all derived from the same basic theological sources that were first produced before the turn of the century. Of course, there is a vast difference in content between liberal and evangelical Sunday School materials, but virtually none between different liberal denominations. They could all have been written by the same people—indeed, perhaps they were.

What follows is a study of The New Curriculum of The United Church of Canada, but it is applicable in general to any liberal Sunday School material, and for this reason should be of interest to a vast segment of church people who are confronted with exactly the same problems.

Seven Accusations

It would be difficult to write any sizeable book without including many things with which everybody would agree, and there are most certainly some fine statements scattered throughout every volume of The New Curriculum. However, there are seven basic fallacies with which the Evangelical Church could never agree and which should raise serious doubts in the minds of those who will study The New Curriculum in the years that lie ahead.

1. It destroys the authority of the Bible.
2. It is intellectually dishonest.
3. It raises problems where there are none.
4. Sometimes it does not mean what it says.
5. It "double-talks" its way through the Virgin Birth and the Second Coming.
6. It confuses faith and works.
7. It proposes universal salvation.

1. *It destroys the Authority of the Bible*

"The Bible was written by human writers who could and did make mistakes. We need not be afraid, when scholars raise questions about the scriptures or point out difficulties in a text, that truth is being distorted or hidden. On the contrary, research and scholarship help us to become aware of various viewpoints, inconsistencies and gaps in the written record. Thus, we sort out the confusions and come closer to the truth" (*Senior Teacher's Guide*, page 289).

In this statement, The United Church of Canada looks for its authority to human reason and science, not to the Bible.

With this principle as a basis, the authors of The

NEW CURRICULUMS

New Curriculum find errors and contradictions from Genesis through Revelation. When they come to the story of Cain and Abel they say, "To express his deep and God-given convictions about God and man he evidently borrowed a traditional tale and revised it to carry his thoughts" (*Senior Teacher's Guide*, page 56). They seem to have no trouble believing that a godly man would manufacture a story and tell it as a fact although he knew that it was not true.

About Noah and the ark, it is rather indignantly suggested, "It is high time that teachers and parents stopped insulting the intelligence of young people by trying to convince them of the literal truth of the Noah story in the face of their commendable scientific attitude toward fact" (*Senior Teacher's Guide*, page 61).

About the Tower of Babel: "For instance, it is hardly factual that at first 'the whole earth had one language' (Genesis 11: 1), or that God deliberately confused the language of all the earth (11: 9) to defeat man's pretensions" (*Senior Teacher's Guide*, page 67).

The story of the Birth of Moses is not fact but fantasy, "Legends, such as the birth story of Moses, are expressions of intuitive insight and religious faith" (*Senior Teacher's Guide*, page 97).

Their account of the plagues in Egypt begins with this sentence, "Efforts to explain these legends as natural events end in failure" (*Senior Teacher's Guide*, page 102). The entire Book of Joshua is transformed into an extremely questionable document by this sentence, "The conquest lasted over several centuries, although reading the Book of Joshua gives the impression that it was the result of a sudden decisive assault" (*Senior Teacher's Guide*, page 128).

With these statements as a background, it is somewhat surprising to find sentences like these:

"No books have ever been so closely scrutinized by able and devoted men as those which we have in the Bible, and today, we are reasonably sure what the original was like" (*God and His Purpose*, page 41).

"Well may we wonder what kind of man he (Jesus) was. The only means we have of knowing comes to us from the Bible . . ." (*God and His Purpose*, page 105).

"If he (Jesus) was neither foolish nor mad, then what he said must be true" (*Senior Teacher's Guide*, page 220).

In these statements, The New Curriculum declares that what Jesus said must be true. The only record we have of Him is the Bible, and we are reasonably sure that our present translations are fairly accurate. When we turn to our only accurate source of knowledge about Jesus, we discover that He believed the story of Cain and Abel, and the account of Noah and the ark. In the Book of Matthew, He refers to both. (Matt. 23: 35, 24: 36–39). He quotes passages from the Books of Moses on many occasions and indicates that He believed Moses wrote them (John 5: 46–47). According to the Curriculum we must accept these words of Jesus as the truth or else we must conclude that He was either foolish or mad. Apparently, The New Curriculum believes the latter, because it does not accept any of these stories as fact.

It is not only the first eleven chapters of Genesis

NEW CURRICULUMS 35

that have suffered from this attack on the authority of the Scriptures, but The New Curriculum approaches the entire Bible with the same perspective. The god of The New Curriculum worships at the shrine of science and bows down before the onslaught of human reason.

2. *It Is Intellectually Dishonest*

It does not surprise us to find The New Curriculum taking the typical Liberal's view of the Creation Story in the Book of Genesis:

"When they turn to the story of Adam and Eve in the garden, they are bound to find it far from believable as a factual account of man's beginnings. A woman made from a rib, and a talking serpent are a bit much to take seriously as scientific fact!" (*Senior Teacher's Guide*, page 50).

"Let it be admitted frankly to them that the story of Adam and Eve bears many signs of primitive folklore" (*Senior Teacher's Guide*, page 52).

"If he considered it factual, today's student surely is justified in calling him (the author of Genesis) a poor scientist" (*Senior Teacher's Guide*, page 51).

"It only serves to keep students out of the church when a teacher continues to wage a campaign for the factual truth of this creation story in the face of such obvious arguments to the contrary" (*Senior Teacher's Guide*, page 74).

"The Bible is not really concerned to answer the question *how* the world has come into being but to proclaim the faith that at the source of the world is God's decision to create it. We are not required to regard such statements as scientific" (*Kindergarten Teacher's Guide*, page 13).

Furthermore, we are not surprised to discover that evolution is the alternative offered to the Genesis account:

"Evolution is just God's orderly way of creating the varied forms of life" (*God and His Purpose*, page 54).

"Evolution must be accepted as a fact, although we are not certain as to how it takes place" (*Senior Teacher's Guide*, page 84).

What does surprise us is that a group of intelligent people have not been honest enough to admit that there is another side to the question of evolution. Any first-year college student should know that even scientists do not look upon evolution as a proven fact but still think of it as a working hypothesis. What some college students do not realize is that there are some eminent scientists who are either sceptical of the entire theory or else accept it only partially. Here is a list, in which every man would come under one of these two categories:

Sir Cecil Wakely—President, Royal College of Surgeons; President, Evolution Protest Movement.

Dr. Basil Atkinson—Librarian of Cambridge University.

Dr. Walter E. Lammerts—Director of Research for Germain's Seed Company, California.

Dr. Warren Weaver—Chairman of the Board of the American Association for the Advancement of Science.

Dr. John W. Klotz—Professor of Biology, Concordia College, St. Louis.

Dr. L. E. Tinkham—Anderson College.

NEW CURRICULUMS

Dr. W. R. Thompson, F.R.S.—Director of Commonwealth Institute of Biological Control, Ottawa; Assistant Director of the Imperial Institute of Entomology.

Dr. R. E. D. Clark—Cambridge University.

Dr. Bales—Professor of Biology, Harding College, Arkansas.

Dr. Duane Gish—Research Chemist at Upjohn Pharmaceutical Company.

Dr. Edward Monsma—Calvin College.

Professor Richard Goldschmidt—University of California.

Professor H. J. Fuller—University of Illinois.

Professor L. J. Stadler—Yale University.

Douglas Dewar, F.Z.S.—British Ornithologist and Barrister-at-Law.

Professor Arthur P. Kelley—Director of the Landenberg Laboratory.

Professor John M. Coulter—University of Chicago.

Professor J. Gray, F.R.S.—Cambridge University.

Rene Dubous—Distinguished Microbiologist.

Herbert Nilsson—Director of the Botanical Institute, Lund, Sweden.

Elliott G. Watson—British Zoologist.

Admittedly, there is a much longer list of eminent scientists who have accepted the evolutionary hypothesis, but with names and positions such as these, intellectual honesty demands that we admit the existence of another position that is held by reliable scientists. Most of the encylopedias are honest enough to do this in connection with their articles on Evolution and Anthropology.

For instance, in *The Encyclopedia Americana* the

article on "Man" includes these statements: "The question as to whether man's body came by such a process of evolution through the animals still remains open.

"Though Zittel gives no fewer than 30 genera of fossil pro-simae and 18 genera of fossil apes, not one connecting link has been found between their hypothetical and ancestral form, and man of the present time. The pithecanthropus erectus, or so-called Trinil man of Java, does not belong to the pedigree of modern man, but to that of the modern apes" (Volume 18, page 182).

The World Book Encyclopedia is written with school children in mind and in the article on "Evolution" the danger of the theory of evolution as far as the Christian position is concerned is pointed out as follows: "If man is in the process of evolving from a lower state, sin tends to become mere imperfection, and the Gospel of redemption from the guilt of sin tends to lose all meaning."

Then the article takes time to indicate the other side of the question: "Some persons also object to the theory of evolution on scientific grounds. Most scientists believe, for example, that the fact that the vertebrates all have many structures on the same plan proves that vertebrates all evolved from some common lower ancestor. But the opponents of the theory believe that this fact merely indicates that the Creator used the same pattern in making species of the same class" (Volume 5, page 334).

Is it not interesting that two secular books that are not intended to teach any sort of religion are honest

NEW CURRICULUMS 39

enough to admit both sides of the question and, is it not a tragedy that a set of books designed to teach the Christian position is so intellectually dishonest that it does not even mention the existence of another position.

Any alert theologian should know that even the evidences of development can be harmonized with the Genesis account on a factual basis without discarding it as myth. There are at least half a dozen ways of doing this. Here are two of them: One might be called Restitutive Creation and has been widely popularized in the Scofield Reference Bible. This theory accepts the evidences of development as all applying to a primitive creation, but teaches that, several thousand years before Christ, God-reconditioned the earth in six literal or Biblical days. "The first creative act refers to the dateless past, and gives scope for all the geologic ages" (*Scofield Reference Bible*, page 3). These ages would fall between the first and second verses of the first chapter of Genesis. The idea is that God first created the heaven and the earth, as in verse one; then, as in verse two, he re-created it.

A second method of harmonizing the facts of science and the Genesis account might be called Progressive Creation. The Progressive Creation school believes that God produced the universe by successive actions of creation, as depicted logically in the first chapter of Genesis, each being followed by a lengthy period of development.

Whether or not one wishes to accept any part of the evolutionary theory and harmonize it with the Genesis account, it is still true that there are scholarly Christians who have done so, and any intellectually honest approach to teaching the Book of Genesis should concede that there are hundreds of people who are quite alert to the facts of modern science but have not found it necessary to throw out the factual aspect of the Creation Story. At least, in this way the Sunday School student has the privilege of choosing for himself after he has heard the whole truth. In The United Church Curriculum he will only hear half the truth. This is intellectual dishonesty.

A second area in which The New Curriculum is intellectually dishonest is to be found in its discussion of the authorship of the Books of the Bible. Here is how the question is presented:

"The text of the first five books of the Bible presents difficulties because of the variety of sources on which it rests. It is the work of devout and able editors, who lived about three or four centuries before Christ" (*Senior Teacher's Guide*, page 101).

About the story of Adam and Eve it says, "It was set down more or less in its present form probably during the reign of Solomon, shortly after 1,000 B.C. The author is known, and yet his name is lost. For convenience, scholars have named him the 'Yahwist' " (*Senior Teacher's Guide*, page 50). From here on, The New Curriculum bases its entire interpretation of the Bible on this *documentary theory* of authorship which concludes that a great deal of the Old Testament was written by three or four different authors, all of whom lived nearly a thousand years after the events about which they wrote. The Curriculum continues to talk about the "Yahwist" as if he was an actual man who

NEW CURRICULUMS

had really lived instead of a hypothetical figure who is nothing more than the result of conjectures based on textual criticism.

If the editors of The New Curriculum had been intellectually honest, they would have admitted that there is a very long list of extremely eminent scholars who have never accepted the *documentary theory* and have always believed that the first five books of the Bible were written almost entirely by Moses and that most of the other Old Testament books were written either by contemporaries or men who lived relatively close to the events.

Here is a partial list of men who have refuted the *documentary theory* and although you will not recognize most of their names, you will be aware of the fact that the institutions with which they are connected are among the best in the world from the standpoint of scholarship. The first four in this list are accepted by all theologians as top-ranking scholars:

Franz Delitzsch—Professor of Theology, University of Leipzig, Germany.

C. Friedrich Keil—Professor of Exegetical Theology and the Oriental Languages, University of Dorpat.

E. W. Hengstengerg—Professor of Theology, University of Berlin.

Theodore Zahn—Professor of Biblical Introduction, Erlangen University, Germany.

H. A. Haevernick—Professor of Theology, University of Konigsberg, Germany.

J. Coppens—Professor of Theology, University of Louvain, France.

W. H. Green—Professor of Oriental and Old Testament Literature, Princeton Theological Seminary.

Benjamin B. Warfield—Professor of Theology, Princeton Theological Seminary.

J. Gresham Machen—Professor of Theology, Princeton and Westminster Theological Seminaries.

Robert D. Wilson—Professor of Old Testament, Princeton Theological Seminary.

James Orr—Professor of Apologetics and Systematic Theology, United Free Church College, Glasgow.

Gerhardus Vos—Professor of Old Testament Theology, Princeton Theological Seminary.

Alexander Heidel—Professor in the Oriental Institute, University of Chicago.

Oswald T. Allis—Professor of Old Testament, Princeton Theological Seminary and Westminster Theological Seminary.

Wilhelm Moeller—Professor Ordinarius of Church History, University of Kiel, Germany.

Merrill Unger—Professor of Semitics and Old Testament, Dallas Theological Seminary.

Edward J. Young—Professor of Old Testament, Westminster Theological Seminary.

M. G. Kyle—Professor in Xenia Theological Seminary, St. Louis, Missouri.

W. L. Baxter—Minister of Cameron, New Brunswick (known for his refutation of Wellhausen's theory).

J. H. Raven—Professor of Old Testament Languages and Exegesis, Theological Seminary of the Reformed Church in America.

When these lists were first published, *The United Church Observer* accused us of relying on "dead experts"

NEW CURRICULUMS

for our authority. It is true that several of these theologians are dead, but we should be aware of the fact that many experts in many fields who are now dead are still considered authorities. I do not know any liberal who does not have his shelves lined with books that were written by men who are now dead.

The fact of the matter is that these "dead men" were alive when these issues were first brought up. They answered them then and their answers are still quite valid, because the issues have not changed. If we were to rob ourselves of the sources whose authors have since died, we would have to throw out more than half of the books in every library.

A little research would reveal that at the time of writing many of these men are still alive and others have died only within the last few years.

It should be remembered, too, that these lists are dreadfully remiss in the names that have been omitted. An exhaustive search would produce eminent names that would fill many more pages. Time and space simply preclude the possibility of noting all the reliable scientists and theologians that hold a conservative position.

If The United Church of Canada wishes to emphasize the *documentary theory* of authorship in the Old Testament, it is free to do so, but if it wishes to be intellectually honest with its Sunday School students, it must admit that there are eminent scholars who do not accept this theory. Then the student can make his own choice after he has heard the whole truth. In The New Curriculum, he will hear only half the truth. This is intellectual dishonesty and should have no place in a Sunday School curriculum for any church.

3. *It Creates Problems Where There Are None*

Many examples of this can be found throughout the Curriculum, but one is sufficient to prove the point. It concerns the crossing of the Red Sea: "How the safe passage was secured for the Israelites while the Egyptians became mired and were drowned is not clear in the narrative. At Exodus 14: 21, two ideas were involved, as you will see if you read the verse in the following two possible orders of its component parts:

" 'Moses stretched out his hand over the sea . . . and the waters were divided' ' . . . and the Lord drove the sea back by a strong east wind all night, and made the sea dry land'.

"Two versions of how the Israelites crossed the Sea of Reeds are involved. One accepts the intervention of God in natural forces as the cause, and the other stresses supernatural powers given to Moses" (*Senior Teacher's Guide*, page 108).

It would seem to me that even a small child would read this passage and see without any difficulty whatever that two aspects of the same event are being described. Moses is pictured as stretching his hand over the sea and God responds to his action by the strong wind which rolled back the sea so that the Children of Israel could pass over on dry land. There is no problem here whatever. It has been created by The New Curriculum.

4. *It Doesn't Always Mean What it Says*

Five examples will be sufficient to demonstrate this:
(1) *Moses and the Burning Bush*—Here is the account

NEW CURRICULUMS 45

as we read it in *God and His Purpose*: "In this mood Moses was arrested by a strange sight, a bush ablaze in the desert, burning and yet still not burned up. He felt God very near to him, so near that he slipped off his sandals in reverence, as men today take off their hats and bow in prayer. God was actually speaking to him" (*God and His Purpose*, page 89).

Any Christian would probably say 'Amen' to this statement. It would seem that the editors of The New Curriculum believe in the facts connected with the story of the Call of Moses. Moses was in the desert. He did see a bush. The bush was on fire, but it was not consumed. Moses actually took his shoes off his feet in reverence and God spoke to him from the burning bush.

This is certainly what the book says, but it is not what The New Curriculum means. When we come to the *Senior Teacher's Guide* we find a different presentation of the same story: "The flaming bush conveys the overpowering presence of the living God. Flames are also involved in the story of Pentecost. The figure of speech of God speaking tells us that Moses knew he was in the divine presence and not in some state of mind he had induced himself. The spoken word means that God's call comes in intelligible ways, and approaches the mind as well as the emotions" (*Senior Teacher's Guide*, page 98).

Thus the account in the Bible becomes unimportant and all we have left is the idea that God impressed Moses in some ambiguous manner which was really quite subjective. When The New Curriculum says that The United Church of Canada believes the story about the

Call of Moses, it does not mean what it says. It believes only that part of it which the mind of man can understand and explain psychologically.

(2) *The Story of the Golden Calf*—If we were to take this account from *God and His Purpose*, it could be included in any Evangelical textbook: "One day when Moses went off into the mountain for communion with God, the people began to think how much easier it was to worship one of the gods they had seen in Egypt. Why not make a god of their own? A golden calf. So they did. Around this image the horrified and dismayed leader found his people, not bowing down in reverent worship, but singing and dancing . . ." (*God and His Purpose*, page 90).

After all the newspaper publicity about The New Curriculum's attitude toward the first eleven chapters of Genesis, we might read this account and believe that now we are on authoritative ground once again. No longer is the Bible a collection of myths and legends. Now that we are beyond the eleventh chapter of Genesis we have left the field of myth and we find ourselves in the area of historical fact.

Unfortunately, such is far from true. Here is how the *Senior Teacher's Guide* treats this incident: "The story of the golden calf is an example of such late writing attributed to the time of Moses.

"This story probably originated at the time of King Josiah in the seventh century, when the conflict over images of bulls to represent Jehovah was at its height. Such images were foreign to the early Israelites, as they were to all the early desert people of Arabia. They were common in Canaanite paganism, and entered Israelite

NEW CURRICULUMS 47

culture after the founding of the monarchy" (*Senior Teacher's Guide*, page 120).

The New Curriculum teaches that this incident did not even take place at all, but was fabricated by an author who lived several hundred years after the Exodus period who inserted this story as if it were history. For most intelligent people, this is a bit too much and creates more problems than it solves. The *Senior Teacher's Guide* makes it apparent that The New Curriculum does not really mean what it says when it tells the story of the golden calf in *God and His Purpose*.

(3) *The Devil*—When we read *God and His Purpose*, it would seem that The New Curriculum teaches the existence of a personal Devil. "He actually called his disciple 'Satan', for it seemed that this idea was the devil himself urging him to give up what was now to be his mission of death" (*God and His Purpose*, page 115).

Of course, it does not really mean what it says about the Devil. The *Senior Teacher's Guide* explains what it does mean: "Do not fall into a pointless argument over the reality of the devil, or of these powers of darkness and light. The New Testament writers expressed their convictions using current imagery, and so do we. Whether there is an actual devil behind the use of the word is not worth discussing" (*Senior Teacher's Guide*, page 297).

(4) *The Resurrection*—If a Sunday School teacher in The United Church tells you that they still believe in the bodily resurrection of the Lord, he can quote statements from The New Curriculum to prove it. For instance: "Hebrew thought refused to surrender the unity of body and spirit. If Jesus was raised

victorious over death, his body had to be 'raised' too—that is to say, his whole person was raised from death, not just the spirit that had inhabited his body. Otherwise there could be no real resurrection. All the references to his bodily presence after the crucifixion stress this point" (*Senior Teacher's Guide*, page 239).

This entire section gives adequate ground for retaining belief in the bodily resurrection of Jesus, but when we come to the *Kindergarten Teacher's Guide*, the resurrection is described quite differently: "The stories in the Gospels that tell of the resurrection of our Lord are strange stories. They are not easily understood . . . Jesus' disciples became aware that he was with them still" (*Kindergarten Teacher's Guide*, page 59).

"The early Christians sensed his presence in three ways:

1. They remembered him as they had known him in his earthly ministry. . . .

2. They knew him also in the present 'leading them into all the truth . . .'

3. But more. He was not only in their past or with them in the present but was ahead of them too as Lord of the future" (*Kindergarten Teacher's Guide*, page 60).

Here then is the real truth about the resurrection. There is little thought of any bodily reality to this event, but instead, we find the resurrection spoken about in the vague language of imagery, impression, and imagination.

Every Christian knows that the Bible itself is quite clear about the bodily resurrection. The authors go to great length to prove the tomb was actually empty and that Jesus was clothed in a body which the disciples were

NEW CURRICULUMS

able to see and touch and one which had the capacity to eat. In some places The New Curriculum says it believes in the bodily resurrection, but it is quite obvious that it does not mean what it says.

(5) *The Miracles*—The authors of The New Curriculum have bent over backwards in an attempt to explain the miracles out of existence. However, in some cases, miracles are accepted without any explanation whatsoever. A good example is the story of Peter and John and the beggar: "A few minutes before he was what he had been since the day he was born, a permanent cripple, resigned to a life of helpless incapacity. Now he was able to get up on his own two feet" (*God and His Purpose*, page 193).

However, we wonder whether the Curriculum really believes in the reality of this miracle when we find a statement such as this: "This is how God intervenes. This is how he cares. He does not stop the ways of the world, but he allows us to share his secrets" (*God and His Purpose*, page 74).

This would lead us to believe that the healing of the beggar was not really a miracle but only a succession of natural events in which God did not have to "stop the ways of the world". In some places the Curriculum seems to say that miracles have actually happened, but after we have read all of the books, we know that they do not really mean what they say. The god of The New Curriculum seems to be impotent when it comes to interrupting his own laws and doing something that is miraculous. If these authors do believe in miracles, then their logic is in grave doubt. Why do they feel that the miracle of the Crossing of the Red Sea had to be explained but the miracle of the healing of the beggar needs no explanation. If God has the power to heal a cripple and make a new man out of him, by what rule of logic do we have to go through the laborious story of the "reeds and the mud" to get the Children of Israel through the Red Sea?

5. *It "Double-talks" Its Way through the Virgin Birth and the Second Coming*

How any thinking person can read The New Curriculum and say that The United Church of Canada still believes in the Virgin Birth of Jesus Christ is a mystery to us. "Modern Christians do not easily accept even the Gospel narratives: Matthew and Luke give different versions, and both can hardly be correct in the matter of Jesus' genealogical tree. The wandering star and the angelic chorus are probably legendary. Is it necessary to believe in the virgin conception of Mary? This may rest on a mistaken translation of Isaiah 7: 14, where the 'young woman' of the original Hebrew became a 'virgin' in the Greek rendering. . . ." Of course, every Bible student knows that the doctrine of the Virgin Birth does not rest on Isaiah 7: 14. This passage can be left out of the Bible and the Gospel narratives still tell the story of a young woman who gave birth to a child who had no human father.

The *Junior Teacher's Guide* continues, "Because of the difficulties, many nowadays would say that no one should be compelled to accept the ideas of the Virgin Birth. Our faith in Jesus Christ is not dependent on them. Nevertheless, I want to add this. The coming of

NEW CURRICULUMS

the Messiah is one of the most wonderful things that ever happened! We must not despise the lovely Gospel stories about the Son of God, *Emmanuel* (God with us). So wonderful is this coming that we must have poetry and picture language to tell forth its meaning, just as we need the inspired paintings of the greatest painters who deal with this theme" (*Junior Teacher's Guide*, page 18). It was probably passages such as this to which Dr. A. W. Ness, Pastor of Toronto's Queensway Cathedral, referred when he said, "The United Church of Canada and, by recent vote, the Baptist Convention of Ontario and Quebec, these two groups have officially gone on record as denying the centre of the Christian faith, the Virgin Birth of Christ."

To this statement *The Observer* replied, "Mr. Ness: That is a lie. That is a nasty, vicious lie about two great churches" (*The Observer*, November 1, 1964, page 36). The truth of the matter is that Dr. Ness' statement is not a lie but it represents the conclusion that any educated person would have to draw from the Curriculum's presentation of the doctrine of the Virgin Birth.

The same issue of *The Observer* contains an article entitled, "The Meaning of Myth", by James Davies. Here is what Mr. Davies says: "The virgin birth did not happen as history and is scientifically impossible, but as a symbol it participates in the truth that God was in Christ reconciling the world unto himself, and therefore, we can still say the Apostles' Creed, 'born of the virgin Mary', and believe in that part of the creed as a symbol and as truth, the truth that Christ was divine" (*The Observer*, November 1, 1964, page 17).

52 PERILOUS TIMES

This is probably the most classic example of "double-talk" we have ever read about any important issue. First he says it cannot happen and then he says we can believe it.

The authors continually talk their way into the Virgin Birth and then back out of it. They have not been courageous enough to say that the birth of Jesus did happen in this manner or to say that it did not happen in this manner. It appears to us that The United Church of Canada does not believe in the Virgin Birth of Jesus Christ, but because it seems afraid to say so in as many words, it proceeds to "double-talk" its way through it.

The same sort of "double-talk" is used in dealing with the Second Coming. "When the risen Lord did not return to Jerusalem in the manner expected by apocalypticism, the influence of this whole framework of ideas began to wane. The imagery of the Little Apocalypse, and similar passages, passed away in the early centuries of the church, after its usefulness was ended. Today such imagery is meaningless to many people, and offensive to others. Yet we must recognize that Jesus used it to express some of his message. It was not allowed to obscure the heart of the gospel—that God's kingdom is a present reality" (*Senior Teacher's Guide*, page 277).

What these sentences really mean, perhaps only the editors of the Curriculum will ever know. Part of this quotation seems to teach that the Second Coming is not to be expected because it is "meaningless to many people, and offensive to others". The next sentence seems to express belief in the Second Coming

NEW CURRICULUMS 53

because "Jesus used it to express some of his message". It reminds us somewhat of the magician's patter. "Now you see it; now you don't."

6. *It Confuses Faith and Works*

"We do not have to know how man's salvation is accomplished by the death and resurrection of Jesus in order to be saved, any more than we must know all about nutrition before we can be fed. We are saved from sin by accepting the fundamental promise that God forgives our sins as we believe in Jesus Christ and forgive others" (*Senior Teacher's Guide*, page 219).

Salvation in this passage is contingent upon two things: (a) Believing in Jesus Christ, and (b) Forgiving others. This is probably based on one of the petitions of The Lord's Prayer: "forgive us our sins; for we also forgive every one that is indebted to us" (Luke 11: 4). This prayer has nothing to do with salvation. It is expressly given for those who are already the children of God. Otherwise, the address "Our Father" is without meaning. The New Testament never makes personal salvation contingent upon a spirit of forgiveness. This spirit is one of the results of the New Birth, not a means to obtain it.

"We cannot doubt that Jesus believed God to be the Father of all men. The fourth gospel states it clearly (John 3: 16)." It is difficult for us to understand what connection there is between the doctrine of the Fatherhood of God and the message of John 3: 16. This verse is offering the entire world a choice between everlasting life and perishing. There is nothing in this entire passage about the Fatherhood of God.

The Curriculum goes on to say, "Sonship with the Father of Jesus Christ depends upon moral responsibility. Men are not sons of God until they turn to him in repentance, seek his forgiveness for their sins (Matt. 6: 12–15), and respond with loving obedience." The Curriculum suggests that Sonship depends upon moral responsibility and then breaks this down into three parts—repentance, seeking forgiveness, and loving obedience. There are many passages in the Word of God which explain how to become a Child of God, but Matthew 6: 12–15 is not one of them. Again this is The Lord's Prayer and is designed for people who are already the children of God. Moral responsibility is never a means to Sonship. It is one of the results.

A final passage from this page of the Curriculum reads as follows: "But man may become a son only by a change of heart, by accepting the discipline of Christ's commands (John 1: 12)" (*Senior Teacher's Guide*, page 226).

Of course, those who are familiar with the Bible know that there is nothing in this verse of Scripture (John 1: 12) that says anything about accepting the discipline of Christ's commands. It talks about becoming a Child of God, and makes it clear that there is only one requirement: ". . . as many as received him, to them gave he power to become the sons of God, even to them that believe on his name."

Such things as obedience, moral responsibility, and forgiveness are never connected with the way of salvation or the manner in which we can become the Children

NEW CURRICULUMS

of God. The Apostle Paul spends a great deal of time in all of his epistles making it clear that no works of ours can possibly result in our salvation. It is all of grace through faith, "Not of works, lest any man should boast" (Eph. 2: 9).

Although there are some passages in The New Curriculum that are Biblically based and seem to make the way of salvation quite clear, other passages such as these which we have quoted confuse the issue of faith and works.

7. *It Proposes Universal Salvation*

The New Curriculum makes a valiant effort to make the Bible say that all men will eventually be saved. "He perceived that Christ was crucified in order that God's love might be brought to all men, in death or in life (Rom. 5: 18; 8: 38–39; 1 Cor. 15: 20–28; Phil. 2: 10–11; 3: 20–21). So certain was he of God's sovereign power and gracious goodness that he dared to hope for the ultimate salvation of all men" (*Senior Teacher's Guide*, page 255).

"Not only do we receive what we get with joy and gratitude, but we take a hand in God's campaign to change the world. We begin to work for a new world in which God's plenty comes to all his children everywhere" (*God and His Purpose*, page 189).

"Its final coming means that no one will be beyond the possibility of redemption (Phil. 2: 9–11; 1 Cor. 15: 22). No evil power will be left unredeemed or undefeated (1 Cor. 15: 25).

"Because Christ's love for us is the ground of our own

hope, so we hope for all men, not just for ourselves" (*Senior Teacher's Guide*, page 282).

"By the church, God carries forward his work of salvation for all mankind. Today this sense of mission is bringing the churches together to realize that beneath all their differences in name and history they are and should be one, at least in spirit and service" (*God and His Purpose*, page 164).

What is the answer to these verses which are used to support the idea of universal salvation? In every case, the conclusion of The New Curriculum is based upon an interpretation or an application that is not correct. When the Bible says that the gift of salvation is available to all men, it does not infer that it will be accepted by all men. The benefits of a gift are never realized until the gift is accepted, and the Bible makes it quite clear that everybody does not accept God's gift. To conclude that they do is not sound Scriptural interpretation.

Sometimes the Curriculum uses verses that obviously apply only to Christians and makes them apply to everybody. This is true of most of the passages that are quoted from the epistles of Paul. Occasionally the word "all" in the epistles of Paul refers to the entire world, but more often to the whole church, all of God's children, or all Believers. When Paul says that nothing "shall be able to separate us from the love of God" (Rom. 8: 39), he is not talking about the whole world. The context of the passage makes it apparent that he has in mind only those who have accepted God's love. It is incorrect to apply this passage to the world. It has nothing whatever to do with the unbeliever, but only

NEW CURRICULUMS

with the Child of God. This is an example of wrong application.

It is this doctrine of Universalism which makes it possible for The New Curriculum to use Dr. Albert Schweitzer as an example of a good Christian, despite the fact that he is a Unitarian. "His writings make it plain that he does not believe in a personal God, petitionary prayer, or any doctrine of atonement, and he is agnostic about life after death" (*Toronto Daily Star*, December 5, 1964, page 15).

The Bible has a great deal to say that completely refutes any idea of Universal Salvation, but all of these passages seem to have been completely ignored by the editors of The New Curriculum. Perhaps one of the best examples is the story of the rich man and Lazarus in the sixteenth chapter of Luke. The whole import of this narrative is that there is no salvation after death for those who have rejected their opportunity in life.

Actually, The New Curriculum is strangely silent on the subjects of Heaven and Hell and Judgment. Any reference to these three things is quite incidental, despite the fact that the Bible concerns Itself with these issues from Genesis through Revelation. There is a Heaven to be gained. There is a Hell to be shunned, and there is a Judgment to be feared. There are some things in the Bible that we do not completely understand, but these things are absolutely clear.

Conclusion

Is it any wonder then that a leading United Church minister says about Evangelical Christians, "I do not speak the same language as these people. Their God is not my God" (*The United Church Observer*, November 1, 1964, page 19). The New Curriculum has manufactured a religion for the Twentieth Century, but why they cling to the name Christian is a mystery to us.

CHAPTER V

THE NEW MORALITY

"AMERICA is the most sex-ridden country in the history of the world. Sex has replaced the Cross as the focus of longing and the image of fulfilment" (*Esquire*, February 1965).

This was the comment of Malcolm Muggeridge during one of his visits to North America. Exactly the same sentiment has been voiced by speakers and writers from coast to coast for the past decade. "Never before in human civilization has sex been so persuasively prostituted to financial gain" (*Christianity Today*, March 12, 1965).

From the Middle Ages to the end of World War I the western world was governed by a rather artificial code of ethics that just did not work. In its latter years it was known as Victorianism.

It adopted a partial Biblical standard because it maintained that sex outside of marriage is sinful. However, it was not in accord with Biblical standards because it inferred that sex within marriage was only for the purpose of producing children and, apart from this, it was considered a sort of dirty activity and a naughty word not to be used in the vocabulary of the average decent citizen. The Roman Catholic Church has been one of the last outposts of Victorianism because of its insistence that any sort of birth control, even within marriage, is not permissible.

The Old Morality created a great many problems.

The Double Standard

A great many men during this period set up one standard of morality for their wives and another for themselves. They expected a girl to enter her marriage a virgin but both before and during the course of his marriage, the average man took advantage of the available "loose women" and prostitutes.

Modesty

It was an age of extreme modesty. Dresses were unbearably long and even bathing suits were made in such a way that no girl could really swim in them. Sometimes they included long sleeves and stockings. A girl's confinement before childbirth was a very realistic thing; particularly during the last months she did not appear in public gatherings and if she went out of her house at all, it was usually simply for a walk after dark.

People did not talk about sex and, of course, it was impossible to read about it. Even as late as 1917 in the United States, it was still unlawful to publish, sell or distribute any book on sex education or instruction.

The Results

The Victorian era created a man's world in which woman was expected to maintain a high standard of morality and stay at home and where man took advantage of "the double standard" and, even if he did not, he entered marriage with little if any knowledge about sex and far too often the results were disastrous.

The New Morality

Dr. Robert W. White, Professor of Clinical Psychology at Harvard University says, "The present situation is a reaction to the excesses of Victorianism" (*Christianity Today*, March 1965).

What is It?

In February of 1965 five hundred ministers and educators met at Harvard University to discuss the implications of the moral problems in the modern world and they described the New Morality in these words, "The right of all persons to some form of sexual enjoyment as soon as they are mature enough to accept the consequences. Where love for the neighbour is safeguarded, any type of behaviour agreed upon by two adult persons is acceptable" (*Christianity Today*, March 1965, page 29).

Dr. Mervyn Dickinson, a Minister of The United Church of Canada, was quoted as consenting to some aspects of the New Morality, "A man should not be condemned for sleeping with another man's wife . . . society, instead, should try to understand the man's motivation of love" (*Toronto Star*, May 27, 1965).

What are the Results?

Already the effects of the New Morality have begun to make a devastating inroad upon family life. In 1870 there was one divorce in thirty-three marriages. In 1964 in the United States there was one divorce in every three marriages.

In addition to these families that have been broken up by divorce, there are countless cases of desertion. In 1953 in the United States $252,000,000 was spent to help abandoned wives and children. Some statistics indicate that every fourth child in the United States does not live with both his parents and that 3,500,000 receive no financial aid whatever from their father.

Illegitimacy

In 1963 in the United States there were 240,200 illegitimate births and 41 per cent of the mothers involved were teenagers. Canada does not stand in any better light. "In view of the mounting number of pregnancies among local students in Manitoba, as well as the alarming rise of venereal disease, Winnipeg's school board has decided to launch a programme of sex education" (*Prairie Overcomer*, December 1964, page 430).

In addition to the breakdown of family life and the increase in illegitimacy, there is a marked increase in the occurrence of social diseases. In 1963 there were 100,000 new cases of venereal disease in the United States. This represented a 72 per cent increase. In Great Britain during the same year there was a 73 per cent increase. These facts become even more alarming when we realize that medical science is now able to cure most of the social diseases without any prolonged and difficult treatment.

Of course, every student of history is well aware of the fact that the morality of our age is not at all new. It has been evident during the decadent years of every great civilization and there are many students of sociology who feel there is a direct link between this kind of morality and the disintegration of a world power.

What was apparent in the Harvard University meeting in February of 1965 was "that the so-called new morality is as old as human evil and its advocacy at least as old as the classical pagan writers" (*Christianity Today*, March 1965, page 30).

The True Morality

Victorianism is not the morality of the Bible and, of course, the New Morality is the complete antithesis of Scriptural ethics.

The Old Testament declares that God made man and woman and sex and said that it was good: "God saw everything that he had made, and, behold it was very good" (Gen. 1: 31).

The writer of the Book of Hebrews sums up the position of the Scriptures in regard to sex in a single verse: "Marriage is honourable in all, and the bed undefiled: but whoremongers and adulterers God will judge" (Heb. 13: 4).

The Bible views sex as one of the good things of God's creation, meant to be enjoyed by mankind, but only within the brackets of the marriage bond.

Professor Paul Ramsey of Princeton says, "The Christian ethic entails a view of marital intimacy . . . that can be justified only within the context of the married state, undertaken with a deep sense of lifelong responsibility" (*Christianity Today*, February 1965).

The Objections

Perhaps the most common excuse of the person who is involved in any sort of immorality is that "everybody does it". The reasoning behind this, of course, is simply that the majority is always right and if a large enough group of people participates in any activity, then it is legitimate for anybody.

In the first place it should be noted that Biblical ethics are not based upon a majority opinion but upon the revelation of God and in most cases they stand in stark contrast to the general morality of any generation. The Christian is almost always forced to go against the stream in every area of his life. He is in the minority and if he lives for God, he must be outside of the world's circle of approval.

In the thirteenth chapter of Matthew Jesus made it quite clear that the majority in this world are headed for destruction and only a minority are on their way to everlasting life. If you maintain Christian principles, in all probability you will be looked upon as an "odd ball" by the world.

It should be remembered, however, that the cliché "everybody's doing it" is not entirely accurate because everybody in fact is *not* doing it. There is a solid core of men and women in this immoral world who are still

THE NEW MORALITY

living in accordance with the moral standards of the Bible so that even if we are in the minority we are never entirely alone.

"But We are in Love"

Some people believe that love justifies any sort of action. Quite often the only defence that teenagers have for their immorality is the naive declaration, "But we are in love"—as if love makes it right to do anything and everything.

Unfortunately, most girls do not know that sex before marriage or outside of marriage is very seldom motivated by love as far as the man is concerned. More often, it is nothing but selfish satisfaction or the desire to put another "notch in his gun" of sexual conquests.

Jennie Loitman Barron, Judge of the Superior Court of Massachusetts, says, "Can sex before marriage be an act of love? Almost never" (*Reader's Digest*, May 1964).

Impossible

At this juncture I can almost see somebody throwing up his hands in despair and exclaiming, "But this is impossible. The Bible holds up a standard of morality that nobody could ever achieve."

And immediately I would have to answer, "Right, right, right!"

The Bible does hold up an impossible standard of morality and it makes it absolutely clear that no man or woman has the strength to either achieve it or maintain it. This is the very purpose for which Jesus

Christ came into the world. Man could do nothing about his own sin and so God had to intervene and provide salvation.

It is when we admit our own helplessness and throw ourselves upon the mercy of God that He comes into our lives and gives us the power that we must have if we are going to live for God.

CHAPTER VI

THE SIN OF SODOM

ACCORDING to the experts every man is a potential homosexual at birth. Whether or not he becomes one depends almost entirely upon his relationship with his parents.

Generally a homosexual is developed by a mother who babies her son to an extreme, over-protects him from rough play with other boys, and guards him from any contact with girls. Some of the psychiatrists think that this sort of mother is having a secret love affair with her son and has let him take the place of her husband whom she has almost completely excluded from her affection.

The father of a homosexual is often a man who has had no time for his son and has commanded very little attention or respect from his wife. If a child has a fairly normal relationship with either one of his parents he will probably have no problem assuming his proper sexual role.

The fact that a boy becomes a homosexual is not his fault, but whether he yields to the temptation to practise perversion is his responsibility.

The "Gay" World

Every large city has its homosexual community or its "gay" world.

The *Kinsey Report* estimated that four per cent of all males over sixteen were homosexuals. Dr. Irving Bieber, Associate Clinical Professor of Psychiatry at the New York Medical College, set his estimate at about two per cent.

The "gay" community has its own bars, beaches, restaurants, barber shops, tailors, gyms, apartment houses, organizations, books, magazines, conventions, and male prostitutes. However, all deviates do not participate in this "gay" life. Some live pretty much to themselves and some marry successfully and have families.

Artistic People

A few extremely clever and creative people have been homosexuals, including Plato, Leonardo da Vinci, Michelangelo, and probably Alexander the Great. Folklore in the "gay" world tries to make out that they are generally very gifted in the arts, but psychiatrists say there is not much evidence to support this idea.

More than eighty-five per cent have no obvious mannerisms. The men are seldom effeminate and the women are not Amazon types. As a matter of fact, even the experts cannot pick them out.

Dr. Paul Gebhard, successor to Dr. Kinsey, says: "More than nine times out of ten a man becomes a homosexual for the sole and simple reason that he cannot help it."

Dr. Irving Bieber says that it is now a treatable condition and he has had a success record of about twenty-seven per cent. In New York City the Homosexual League asked three hundred deviates, "Would

THE SIN OF SODOM

you want to be cured if you could?" Ninety-six per cent answered, "No."

From all sides comes the conclusion that a homosexual is an extremely lonely person who has difficulty living in a heterosexual world and seeks an escape by surrounding himself with people who are similarly afflicted.

Extermination of Perverts

In the Old Testament it was one of a number of sins that bore the death penalty. It is listed along with adultery, sacrificing children to idols, intercourse with animals, consulting spirit mediums, and cursing parents (Lev. 18 and 20).

In each case the penalty was death. "If a man also lie with mankind, as he lieth with a woman, both of them have committed an abomination: they shall surely be put to death; their blood shall be upon them" (Lev. 20: 13).

In the New Testament it is still listed as a sin. Death is still the penalty, but it is to be executed by God in the next world. "For this cause God gave them up unto vile affections: for even their women did change the natural use into that which is against nature: And likewise also the men, leaving the natural use of the woman, burned in their lust one toward another; men with men working that which is unseemly, and receiving in themselves that recompence of their error which was meet. Who knowing the judgment of God, that they which commit such things are worthy of death" (Rom. 1: 26, 27, and 32).

The same principle is clearly taught in the Corinthian

Epistle: "Don't you know that those doing such things have no share in the kingdom of God? Don't fool yourselves. Those who live immoral lives—who are idol worshippers, adulterers, or homosexuals—will have no share in His kingdom" (1 Cor. 6: 9-10, "Living Letters").

The Worst Sin?

In both Old and New Testaments the sin of perversion is listed with a great many other sins. It is not isolated and put into a class by itself.

The passages cited in Leviticus, Romans and Corinthians include it in the same category as adultery, offering children to idols, intercourse with animals, consulting spirit mediums, cursing parents, fornication, covetousness, maliciousness, envy, murder, deceit, backbiting, atheism, pride, egotism, disobedience to parents, covenant breaking, idolatry, stealing, and drunkenness.

The teaching of the Bible is that "The wages of sin is death." Spiritual death is the penalty for all sin. There may be some Biblical authority to conclude that there will be degrees of punishment but these are usually related to the amount of light and opportunity a man has had, not to the baseness of his sin. The Bible does not couple adultery, perversion, and murder in one passage and covetousness, pride, and jealousy in another as if the former were more heinous than the latter. Sin is simply bundled together and its final outcome is separation from God or the second death.

THE SIN OF SODOM

Let's Be Lenient

The British Wolfenden Report says in part: "Homosexual behaviour between consenting adults in private should no longer be a criminal offence . . . there must remain a realm of private morality and immorality which is, in brief and crude terms, not the law's business."

Whether we like this or not, it is true that personal morals of adults cannot be adequately controlled by the State and they are basically a matter between a man and his God. If a homosexual is not a Christian, he is doomed to spend eternity in hell anyway and refraining from his perversion will not save him from that destiny.

We Can't Be Lenient

The Church can never be lenient where God is not lenient. We may convince ourselves that homosexuality is a sickness, but the Bible says it is sin.

"They can't help it," objects the liberal minister or theologian. But even some psychiatrists who have no religious flag to wave are willing to admit that these people can be treated and helped. Add to this the transforming power of the Gospel and the Christian can be extremely optimistic.

If the Gospel cannot meet the need of a pervert, then we have no reason to expect it to meet the need of an adulterer or liar or thief. The history of the Christian Church has proved the power of Jesus Christ to deliver from *all* sin, including the practice of homosexuality.

The real issue here is not the ability of God but the willingness of the deviate to avail himself of God's power and forgiveness and cleansing.

Marriage for Perverts

Canada was shocked recently when *The United Church Observer* printed an article by Rev. Mervyn Dickinson suggesting that the church might arrange to solemnize the marriage of homosexuals.

Apart from the Bible, psychiatrists are not at all agreed that homosexuals can maintain a successful marriage. Dr. Irving Bieber says: "Homosexuals get some satisfaction, but are probably never fulfilled." He points out that their relations with each other are turbulent and short-lived, seldom more than a year or two. If this is true, then marriage is out of the question apart from Biblical morality.

If the church could sanctify adultery or stealing or idolatry or intercourse with animals or atheism or pride, then it could solemnize the marriage of homosexuals.

To do these things we would have to obliterate our conception of sin. If we renounced our idea of sin, we would have to throw away our Bible. If we threw away our Bible, we would have no authority for any Christian Church.

This is just one more evidence of the fact that the religion of the liberals is not Christianity. It is the religion of the Antichrist.

THE SIN OF SODOM

Some Pertinent References

1. "Speaking Frankly on a Once Taboo Subject", Irving Bieber, *New York Times Magazine*, Aug. 23, 1964, p. 75 (Associate Clinical Prof. of Psychiatry, N.Y. Medical College).
2. "New York's 'Middle-Class' Homosexuals", Wm. J. Helmer, *Harper's*, March 1963, p. 85.
3. "Homosexuality in America", Bill Eppridge and Ernest Havemann, *Life*, June 26, 1964, p. 66.
4. "Homosexuals and the Campus", Charles Young, *His*, Feb. 1966, p. 14.
5. "The Church and the Homosexual", Mervyn Dickinson, *United Church Observer*, Nov. 15, 1965, p. 22.
6. *The Erotic Revolution*, Lawrence Lipton, Sherborne Press Inc., Los Angeles, California.
7. *Crisis in Morality*, C. W. Scudder, Broadman Press, Nashville, Tennessee, p. 31.

CHAPTER VII

THE BIBLE AND INTEGRATION

FOUR obscure passages in the Old Testament seem to support the theory of an inferior race, but the major teaching of the Bible drives home the truth of human equality and opportunity. It was probably Jesus who staged the first "sit-in" when He ignored the custom of His day and ate with an inferior breed called "publicans and sinners".

Before we discuss these Bible statements which seem to contradict each other, we should remind ourselves of some of the world's racial statistics. Sociologists usually divide the world into three major races. The Mongoloids, or yellow peoples, represent thirty-four per cent; the Caucasoids, or whites, represent fifty-six per cent; the Negroids, or blacks, make up the remaining ten per cent.

There are approximately 210,000,000 Negroid people in the world today—three-quarters of them live in Africa, 24,000,000 in South America, 19,000,000 in the United States, 125,000 in Europe, and 30,000 in Canada.

In our time, Negroes have become increasingly prominent in many different fields of endeavour. Benjamin O. Davis became a Brigadier General in the United States Army, and his son became a Major General in the United States Air Force during the Second World War. In 1928 Oscar Depriest became the first Negro Congressman. In 1947 Jackie Robinson

THE BIBLE AND INTEGRATION

became the first major league ball player. In 1950 Ralph Bunche became the first Negro to win the Nobel Peace Prize. In 1955 Marian Anderson became the first Negro to sing in the Metropolitan Opera. In 1957 Althea Gibson became the first Negro to win the Women's Singles in tennis at Wimbledon. Other Negroes have continued to prove to the world that they are not inferior when given a chance to develop.

There is no racial problem in any country until there is a considerable percentage of two different races living together. The most severe problem in the world is in South Africa. When I was there in 1960 there was one European to three Bantus. When this problem explodes it will make the present struggle in the United States seem like a very small drop in a very large bucket, and the contents of the bucket in this case will be blood.

In the United States there is one coloured person to approximately ten white people. This is a serious ratio and is creating struggle and violence from coast to coast. In Canada there is probably one coloured person to every 500 white people. Thus, Canadians are in no position to criticize either the United States or South Africa. At the present time we can observe racial tension so objectively that it is unreal.

Probably the best test of your personal views about integration is the marriage test. Where there is integration there will always be inter-racial marriages. When our soldiers occupied Germany they married German girls. When American soldiers occupied Japan and Korea they married Japanese and Korean girls. History has proved that Negroids can fall in love with

Caucasoids and Caucasoids can fall in love with Mongoloids. Romance is no respecter of races.

If you are a Jew, you should ask yourself the question, "Do I want my daughter to marry a Gentile?" If the answer is no, then you do not really believe in integration.

If you are a Japanese, you should ask the question, "Do I want my son to marry a European?" If the answer is no, then you do not believe in integration.

If you are a Negro, you should ask the question, "Do I want my daughter to marry a white man?" If the answer is no, then you do not really believe in integration.

Probably the biggest battle that we will ever fight about the problem of integration is the battle of marriage. Until we have accepted the idea that integration and inter-marriage go together, we are still fighting the preliminary skirmishes.

When I was in South Africa in 1960 I visited one of the native compounds near Kimberley. The European overseer took time to explain the theological position behind Apartheid. It is based on four rather obscure passages in the Old Testament.

After Ham had seen the nakedness of his inebriated father, Noah, he was cursed in these words: "Cursed be Canaan; a servant of servants shall he be unto his brethren. And he said, Blessed be the Lord God of Shem; and Canaan shall be his servant" (Gen. 9: 25–26).

The tenth chapter of Genesis tells us that among others, the Jebusites, the Amorites, and the Hivites were the descendants of Ham through his son Canaan. This group camouflaged themselves in such a way that

THE BIBLE AND INTEGRATION

they were able to make peace with Joshua before he slew them, and instead of killing them he further cursed them in these words, "Now therefore ye are cursed, and there shall none of you be freed from being bondmen, and hewers of wood and drawers of water for the house of my God" (Joshua 9: 23).

The fact that these people were the dark-skinned peoples of the world may have been inferred from the first chapter of The Song of Solomon where the girl in question describes herself as a dark-skinned servant. She may have been one of the descendants of Ham and Canaan who was still allowed to live in the land. She laments: "Look not upon me, because I am black, because the sun hath looked upon me: my mother's children were angry with me; they made me the keeper of the vineyards; but mine own vineyard have I not kept."

Whether this is good exegesis or not, certainly the book of Genesis condemns some nations to a life of servitude and this girl in Solomon's life was very much like modern African natives—she worked for someone else and perhaps had no vineyard of her own.

Another problem with this theology is whether or not modern man is expected to help God along with this curse by seeing to it that the black man remains a servant, or whether God could conceivably do it without our help. Certainly, this curse is not reiterated or even referred to in the New Testament. Slavery seems to be accepted by the New Testament writers as the status quo, but the thrust of the message is the unity of all kinds of men into the brotherhood of faith in Jesus Christ. Of course, most of the slaves in the Roman Empire period were white men.

This is the case for inequality, and it depends upon the dubious interpretation of a difficult passage. The case for equality and human dignity can be derived from a multitude of verses and there is no question about their interpretation. Here are a few of the highlights:

In the Book of Psalms, David stresses the importance of dwelling together: "Behold, how good and how pleasant it is for brethren to dwell together in unity!" (Psalm 133: 1).

The Book of Proverbs reminds us that we are equal in creation. "The rich and poor meet together: the Lord is the maker of them all" (Prov. 22: 2).

The Prophet Malachi sets forth the same principle in stronger language: "Have we not all one father? hath not one God created us? why do we deal treacherously every man against his brother?" (Mal. 2: 10).

In the Book of Matthew Jesus confirms the teaching of the Old Testament: "For one is your Master, even Christ; and all ye are brethren. And call no man your father upon the earth: for one is your father, which is in heaven" (Matt. 23: 8 & 9).

The Gospel of Mark broke the story of the first "sit-in". Apparently the area where the publicans and sinners lived was out of bounds for Jews, and the Pharisees were horrified to find Jesus flagrantly defying this custom: "When the scribes and Pharisees saw him eat with publicans and sinners, they said unto his disciples How is it that he eateth and drinketh with publicans and sinners?" (Mark 2: 16).

There were no "coloured" or "white" drinking fountains in the days of Jesus but everybody seemed to know that Jews and Samaritans just did not drink from

THE BIBLE AND INTEGRATION

the same bottle—that is, everybody but Jesus. In the fourth chapter of John the Samaritan woman was stunned when this Jewish teacher asked her for a drink: "How is it that thou, being a Jew, askest drink of me, which am a woman of Samaria? for the Jews have no dealing with the Samaritans" (John 4: 9).

After listening to the teaching of Jesus for three years, the Apostle Peter was still slow to accept the doctrine of equality. It was only after an unusual vision that Peter saw the light and told Cornelius, "Ye know how that it is an unlawful thing for a man that is a Jew to keep company, or come unto one of another nation; but God hath shewed me that I should not call any man common or unclean" (Acts 10: 28).

The Apostle Paul preached this same truth to the philosophers in Athens: "God that made the world and all things therein hath made of one blood all nations of men for to dwell on all the face of the earth" (Acts 17: 26).

The Bible says that the blood that flows through the veins of the Southern segregationist is exactly the same as the blood that flows through the veins of the Southern share-cropper.

There are other passages that set forth the same principles and it is obvious even to the casual reader that the Bible teaches equality and human dignity. What then do we do with the Old Testament verses that seem to give a basis for racial inferiority?

There is a basic rule of Bible Study that says, "Never interpret a clear passage in the light of an obscure passage, and never interpret an obscure passage in a manner that contradicts the teaching of a number of clear passages." There is no doubt in any one's mind that the passages that seem to support the idea of an inferior race are extremely obscure and to arrive at the idea of an inferior race from these depends upon a series of human assumptions. It is quite apparent that in the light of scores of clear passages throughout the entire Bible, it would be absolutely wrong to try to teach racial inferiority from the Bible.

Equality and human rights are stressed again and again. The idea of an inferior race, and therefore second-class citizenship, does not have a scriptural leg to stand on.

CHAPTER VIII

THE BIBLE—DO I KNOW THE AUTHOR?

IT adds interest and sometimes authority to any book if you know the author or at least know something about him. When I had finished reading an exhaustive two volume biography of Charles Dickens I immediately dusted off my copies of *David Copperfield* and *Oliver Twist* and re-read them as though I had never seen them before.

A book on child psychology would be somewhat ineffective if you were to discover that the author had never been married and had no children of his own. A volume of war stories would lose the ring of authenticity if you were to learn that the author was a pacifist. An excellent treatise on homiletics would have little value if it had been written by a university professor who had spent his life in a theological seminary rather than behind a pulpit. Certainly a brilliant writer can often handle subjects with which he has had no personal experience, but there is an added authority to his work if he has been there himself.

This principle holds true of the books of the Bible as far as their human authorship is concerned. Knowing the facts of David's life will stimulate your interest in his Psalms. Familiarity with the rather fragmentary account of the episodes in the career of the Apostle John will give you a greater appreciation of his Gospel and his Epistles. Many of the verses in the Pauline letters are brought into sharp relief by a knowledge of his background.

All of this is quite true but it applies to any book, and although it adds interest and authority if you know the writer, it is by no means a necessity.

Most of the authors you have never met in person and you know very little about them. However, their writings accomplish their main purpose. You get their message or are inspired by their thoughts or are entertained by their story. You can understand the average book without knowing the author.

As opposed to all other books, the Bible claims that until you do know the Author you cannot know the Book. If you want to understand the Bible you must be acquainted with the Divine Author of the Bible. You must have that personal knowledge of God that comes when a man trusts Jesus Christ as his Saviour, enters into the experience of the new birth, and becomes a member of the family of God. When this happens you are given a spiritual eyesight that is essential to a study of the Bible.

"As it is written, Eye hath not seen, nor ear heard, neither have entered into the heart of man, the things which God hath prepared for them that love him.

"But God hath revealed them unto us by his Spirit; for the Spirit searcheth all things, yea, the deep things of God.

"For what man knoweth the things of a man, save the spirit of man which is in him? even so the things of God knoweth no man, but the Spirit of God.

"Now we have received, not the spirit of the world,

THE BIBLE

but the spirit which is of God; that we might know the things that are freely given to us of God.

"Which things also we speak, not in the words which man's wisdom teacheth, but which the Holy Ghost teacheth; comparing spiritual things with spiritual.

"But the natural man receiveth not the things of the Spirit of God: for they are foolishness unto him: neither can he know them, because they are spiritually discerned" (I Cor. 2: 9-14).

The Eyes of an Artist

I walked through the massive cold halls of The Louvre and stood like an obedient tourist before a huge canvas made thick and heavy with many coats of different coloured oils. It was the work of one of the greatest masters of all time. I looked at it eagerly but saw nothing. It was no more impressive or important than the coloured print reproduced by some unknown commercial artist that hung in calendar form on a wall in our kitchen. Actually, as far as I was concerned, the calendar was more interesting than the painting in The Louvre.

There was a young woman sitting on a high stool in front of the masterpiece. The pallet and the small easel labelled her as an art student. She was looking intently at the great canvas before her. Occasionally she would make a few bold strokes with her brush on her own little canvas. Then she would look again. I watched her for a long time. She seemed to be absolutely oblivious to the dozens of tourists surrounding her.

There was a glow of rapture in her rather dreamy eyes. Her whole being was captivated by the master's work.

I backed off, moved to one side, walked up close, shut my eyes, and then opened them again hoping that I might be able to see what she saw, but I failed. It was still just a huge piece of canvas stretched on a massive frame and covered with great splashes of coloured paint.

She had the eyes of an artist. I did not. I looked but I did not see. I am not an artist.

The Eyes of Memory

Occasionally I drive through the district where I lived as a boy. I show my family the streets where I played, the trees I used to climb, the corner store where I shopped for my one-cent candy, the field where I played "Cops and Robbers", but to them it all means very little. They look out of respect for me, but they fail to see anything unusual. I look through the eyes of my boyhood experiences and I can see. They have not shared in those experiences, they do not have the same eyes, and they cannot see.

The Eyes of the Soul

The Apostle Paul says that you need to have the eyes of your soul opened if you want to see the things of God. The natural man can see natural things. He can see the Book, read the print on the page, and follow the story, but he cannot understand the message until the Spirit of God gives him spiritual eyesight.

THE BIBLE

It takes the eyes of the artist to appreciate great art, the ears of the musician to understand fine music, the heart of personal experience to be excited over boyhood haunts, and it takes the eyes and ears and heart of the soul opened by the Spirit of God to understand the wonders of the Word of God.

Jesus told Nicodemus that unless he was born again he would not be able to see the kingdom of God, and without doing violence to the teaching of Scripture we could read that verse stopping after the word "see". "Except a man be born again he cannot see."

Without the spiritual eyesight that comes with the new birth no man can see spiritual things and therefore cannot even begin to be a student of the Word of God. The Bible says: "Study to shew thyself approved unto God, a workman that needeth not to be ashamed, rightly dividing the word of truth." Before you begin your study of the Bible ask yourself the question, Do I know the Author? An unsaved person can search the Bible to find the way of salvation, but any further understanding of God's Word is absolutely impossible until he knows the Author personally and the miracle of regeneration has opened the eyes of his soul. "Except a man be born again he cannot see."

CHAPTER IX

THE BIBLE—DO I KNOW THE MEANING?

ALL Scripture has just one basic meaning. You do not know your Bible until you are clear on this. Each verse says one thing—not two or three, but just one.

Many sincere students of the Word are carried away with the spiritual applications or the prophetic significance of a passage before they have learned what the verses actually say. The second chapter of The Book of Revelation is an excellent example of this: "Unto the angel of the church of Ephesus write; These things saith he that holdeth the seven stars in his right hand, who walketh in the midst of the seven golden candlesticks;

"I know thy works, and thy labour, and thy patience, and how thou canst not bear them which are evil: and thou hast tried them which says they are apostles, and are not, and hast found them liars:

"And hast borne, and hast patience, and for my name's sake hast laboured, and hast not fainted.

"Nevertheless I have somewhat against thee, because thou hast left thy first love" (Rev. 2: 1-4.)

These verses and those following present a great temptation to the zealous student. Either he will begin immediately to dig out the many heart-searching applications of these chapters or else he will pull up his

THE BIBLE

Biblical landing gear and sail off into the stratosphere of prophetic interpretation. This is all quite in order as long as he has taken time first of all to find out what the passage actually says apart from applications or prophetic significance.

If he does not know the basic meaning his applications are quite likely to be completely unfounded and his prophetic interpretation a mere figment of his overzealous imagination.

Meaning and Principle

There is nothing very profound about the meaning of this particular passage, but it is important to the rest of our study that we know it. The inspired writer says that there is a Christian church at Ephesus. There are real live people in that church. They have some good spiritual characteristics and they have one outstanding fault. Jesus sends this message through His servant John commending them for their works, labour, patience, orthodoxy, and sacrifice, and rebuking them for their lack of love for the Lord. This is the basic meaning of the passage and everything else stems from this.

In connection with the basic meaning there is always a basic principle being set forth. Probably there are not more than a score of great basic truths set forth in the Bible all the way from Genesis through Revelation. These foundation facts appear again and again and they never change. The passage of time, the advent of a new dispensation or the progress of the world do not change these basic foundation truths of the Bible.

They are the same in The New Testament as in The Old Testament, the same in the Age of Grace as in the Age of Law.

The applications and illustrations and descriptions are important but they should never be allowed to overshadow or contradict the fundamental truths.

Love for God

The verses we have just quoted from Revelation state again a truth that is paramount in the Bible, that love for God holds the pre-eminent place among all the virtues of God's people. This is what the passage says. This is what it means. In the course of saying this many other good things are also said, but if we learn these other less important things and fail to see this basic principle we are not "rightly dividing the word of truth".

In the third chapter of First Peter we find the concluding seven verses of a long discussion about submission. Peter has been talking about submission to authority under three captions—the state, the employer, and the husband. In the course of discussing the last of these he talks about ladies' clothing and hair styles and jewelry. However, these verses were not written to tell Christian women how they should dress but rather the spirit of submission with which they should live with their husbands.

It is quite possible to read this passage and be sidetracked by the illustration Peter uses to emphasize his basic message and fail to see the message itself. Some people do this with the whole Bible. They

THE BIBLE

know all the incidentals of Scripture and none of the fundamentals.

The Danger of Illustrations

This is the danger of good illustrations in a sermon. Sometimes the story is so striking that the people miss the point. I occasionally use an illustration about Model T Fords that I feel is one of the best God has ever given me. Not long ago I repeated the Model T story in my own church on a Sunday morning. The congregation seemed to be listening intently. After the service I stopped to chat with some of our teenage boys. They congratulated me enthusiastically about the sermon. This does not happen very often among people of this age group and often it makes one wonder if they understand any of the preaching. Needless to say I was thrilled with their reaction. I thought, At last I have got through to them. After all these years their attention has been arrested. Then one of them broke the balloon, "We were so interested in your morning message that we have agreed to go out and buy a Model T Ford."

They had heard the story but they had not heard the application. They were interested in the Model T but they had missed the truth I was trying to proclaim. The illustration had become more important than the point.

It is easy to make the mistake of concentrating on the Model T Fords of the Bible. Some people know nothing else, but we are not real students of the Word of God unless we have learned the basic meanings and have been saturated with the fundamental truths of the Book.

"Study to shew thyself approved unto God a workman that needeth not to be ashamed, rightly dividing the word of truth." This necessitates an answer to the question, Do I know the basic meaning?

CHAPTER X

THE BIBLE—DO I KNOW THE APPLICATION?

AFTER you are familiar with the basic meaning and fundamental principles of a passage you can begin to consider the applications. Each verse in the Bible has only one meaning but it may have many applications.

Important doctrines should be based upon the meaning and fundamental principles set forth, not upon one of the many applications. Sermons for the purposes of inspiration, exhortation, and illustrative teaching are usually developed from the applications of Scripture, granted that the actual meaning has been taken into consideration. If the meaning is not clear the application may be entirely unfounded.

We have already noted the historical meaning of the first four verses of the second chapter of Revelation, but we will miss a great blessing if we do not search these verses for their applications to our lives and our churches.

Modernism

There is a sermon here on modernism and false teaching. "Thou hast tried them which say they are apostles, and are not, and hast found them liars." The actual meaning of these words leaves us with a picture of a church that existed nearly two thousand years ago that met and dealt with false teachers. If we conclude our study at this point, we will not get much help from this passage for our own lives. When we carry this situation forward through the centuries and see ourselves and our modern churches in the same picture we are making an application of Scripture. Although this passage does not actually refer to us it does apply to us, and it is quite in accordance with logical Bible study to make this application.

Backsliding

There is another sermon here about backsliding. "Thou hast left thy first love." These are the climatic words of this entire passage and although their meaning takes us back over the centuries to a church in Asia whose members have long since gone to be with their Lord and their problem of backsliding is now ancient history, nevertheless the application of this basic truth can be used in any age and among any group of people who have experienced a retrogression in their Christian experience.

Revival

You have heard many sermons from these verses on Revival. The meaning gives us a picture of a church in history that needed revival. The application will take this historical picture and transform it into a modern photograph. When this happens the Church of Ephesus gradually fades out and is replaced by our own church. Those Christians of bygone days walk off the scene and we move out to take their places. The name of the church is different and the personalities are changed but the basic problems and needs are exactly the same.

THE BIBLE

It is at this point that the Bible begins to be a blessing to us. The historical meaning may leave us cold and indifferent, but if we allow the Spirit of God to make the application the words come to life.

"Study to shew thyself approved unto God, a workman that needeth not to be ashamed, rightly dividing the word of truth."

Until we have seen the application of Scripture to our own lives and times we have not done a thorough job of study. After you have answered the question, Do I know the meaning? ask yourself the question, Do I know the application?

CHAPTER XI

THE BIBLE—DO I KNOW THE PROPHETIC SIGNIFICANCE?

IN addition to the basic meaning and application some passages of Scripture may have a prophetic significance. Each verse has just one meaning. It usually has many applications, and it may have some prophetic significance.

The third chapter of Revelation has all three. We have already noted the meaning of the first four verses and we have discussed three of the many possible applications. Our study of this section of the Bible will not be complete until we see the prophetic significance.

The meaning involves a church in ancient Asia called Ephesus made up of a group of Christians who had lost their first love and were rebuked for it by the Lord. The applications that we have seen concern false teachers, backsliding, and revival. The prophetic significance paints these verses on a much larger canvas than the picture of either the Ephesian Church or the Modern Church and we see them prophetically as a part of a huge panorama of the Christian Church from her inception to the coming of her Lord in all of her varying stages.

We miss some of the blessing if we do not see this forward look of Scripture because in many passages the Bible speaks not only historically and currently but

THE BIBLE

also with an unerring eye upon the future. We call this forward look prophecy in the common sense of the term.

Prophetic Fanatics

It is important in this connection to know that all Scripture does not have a prophetic significance. There is a great deal of prophecy in the Bible, but the Bible is not all prophecy. Much of it is historical or current and nothing more. Some students of the Word have allowed themselves to dwell so consistently upon the prophecy of the Bible that they have become prophetic fanatics.

For this kind of person everything in the Bible is a prophecy of a future age. They focus their prophetic binoculars at the first verse of Genesis and do not remove them until they have reached the last verse of Revelation. Their Bible Class teaching is always prophetic. Their evangelistic sermons are prophetic. Their radio broadcasts are prophetic.

The prophetic fanatic usually feels that almost every thing in the present or any future age was prophesied in the Bible, and they go to great lengths to find automobiles and aircraft and atomic bombs and earth satellites in the pages of the Word of God. This is interesting but by no means necessary and in many instances impossible. Most of these things are not mentioned at all in the Bible and we can only infer them from a few obscure passages and then only after we have done exegetical hand-springs.

The Bible is no less the Word of God if it does not mention hydrogen bombs or space travel any more than it would be considered less inspired because it did not refer to automatic toasters and vacuum cleaners. The prophetic significance is fascinating, encouraging, stimulating, and instructive, but there is no need to labour the point. There is sufficient prophecy without making everything prophecy.

Blinded by Prophecy

We should avoid the danger of concentrating on prophecy to such an extent that we miss the personal message. What a spell-binding picture John paints in Revelation of the whole Christian church in terms of the situation and the problems in the seven churches of Asia! But what a tragedy if we are so fascinated by the prophetic picture that we miss the personal application!

It is very easy to see the Church of Ephesus as symbolic of the Christian Church in its young spiritual days but in the first stages of spiritual regression because of its loss of love for the Lord, and become so wrapped up in this that we fail to hear the voice of the Spirit of God saying, "This is not just a description of a historical church or a type of a prophetic church. This is an analysis of your personal need. You have left your first love and you need to get right with God."

One Purpose of Prophecy

If our study of the coming of the Lord does not result in a life of greater purity and more ardent service, we have missed the point of prophecy. When John describes the hope of the Christian in the second coming

THE BIBLE

of Christ he hastens to add "And every man that hath this hope in him purifieth himself, even as he is pure" (I John 3: 3).

I have attended Prophetic Conferences where some of the finest teachers on the subject have dealt with almost every hair in the tails of the Apocolyptic horses but have failed to make the important connection between prophetic truth and world evangelization.

We can bask in the warm sun of prophecy for days and as long as we look at it objectively and impersonally as a sort of Biblical science our way of life will never be changed. If we allow the Spirit of God to make the connection between prophetic truth and Christian responsibility, then there must be action and prayer and sacrifice.

It is important that we draw a line between the danger of becoming prophetic fanatics and the error of remaining prophetic ignoramuses. "Study to shew thyself approved unto God, a workman that needeth not to be ashamed, rightly dividing the word of truth." Until we have searched for the prophetic significance of a passage we have not done a good job of studying.

We have asked the questions, Do I know the Author? Do I know the meaning? Do I know the application? Now we should ask the question, Do I know the prophetic significance?

CHAPTER XII

THE BIBLE—DO I KNOW THE CONTEXT?

IT is not wrong to take a text out of its context. Some of the finest sermons are based upon passages that have been deliberately removed from their setting in the Bible. When this is done two rules must be observed: (1) A text out of context cannot be used if in its new setting it contradicts the rest of the Bible. (2) A text out of context should not be used as the basis of an important doctrine unless other passages in their context teach the same truth.

Atheism

It is not wrong to use a text out of context but we need to be very careful for there are many dangers in doing so. If we allow ourselves to remove passages from their Biblical setting we can support almost any belief from the Word of God. The atheist can base his godless life on the Bible. The Book of Psalms says quite clearly, "There is no God" (Ps. 15: 1). Of course, everyone knows that this is just a phrase of the Bible out of context. Put it back where it belongs and instead of supporting atheism it condemns it. "The fool hath said in his heart, There is no God."

Polytheism

Polytheism can be taught from the Bible, "The gods are come down to us in the likeness of men" (Acts 14:

THE BIBLE

11). However, if we put these words back into the story from which they were taken we see immediately that this was a conclusion to which the people of Lystra came after Paul and Barnabas had healed the impotent man, and Paul rebuked them for it.

Important Decisions

We can support almost any decision in life if we are content to read and apply the Word of God out of context. I have known people who let their Bibles fall open where they will, drop their hands on the page, read the verse upon which their fingers rest, and then go out and do what it says. This they call the leading of the Lord.

The classical example of this is the man who used this method and was led to the fifth verse of the twenty-seventh chapter of Matthew, "Then Judas went and hanged himself." This failed to help him and he tried again. The second time he was led to read the thirty-seventh verse of the tenth chapter of Luke, "Go and do thou likewise." In desperation he made one more attempt and came to the twenty-seventh verse of the thirteenth chapter of John, "That thou doest, do quickly." Here is suicide based on a text-out-of-context approach to Bible reading combined with an immature Christian's method of deciding what to read.

There was the man who tried to choose his business partner and used this childish method to find the leading of the Lord. One good possibility was crossed off the list when his finger happened to fall on a verse that commanded, "Have thou nothing to do with that just man" (Matt. 27: 19). Of course, the verse has nothing to do with business partners. These are the words of Pilot's wife urging him to release Jesus.

Then there was the husband who had been beset by his wife to buy her a watch for her birthday. He did not know what to do and he decided to go to the Bible and see if God would help him make the decision. Instead of a systematic adult approach he used the fortune teller's method and let his finger fall unguided on a verse. There was the answer directly from heaven, "Ye have a watch" (Matt. 27: 65). Put these words back where they belong and even a child can see that they have nothing to do with a time-piece. This watch was the guard to surround the tomb of Jesus and prevent his disciples from stealing the body.

Finally, there was the woman who thought she needed a new washing machine, but she was afraid to ask her husband lest he refuse to buy it. Her Bible fell open, her hand descended, and she had the answer, "Go ye rather to them that sell, and buy for yourselves" (Matt. 25: 9). Return these violated verses to their own story and they have nothing whatever to do with this woman's problem.

Spiritual Immaturity

There is a distressingly large number of Christians who use this method almost every day in the trivial and important decisions of their lives. It is true that occasionally God seems to overlook their spiritual immaturity and helps them to make the right decisions despite their stupidity, but how much better to have

THE BIBLE

a mature working knowledge of the great principles of the Bible so that every decision of life will be based upon these truths which constitute the foundation of Christian living.

Important decisions should never be determined by ridiculous violations of the meaning of Scripture applied completely out of its Divine context. This is a method for spiritual babies, and I think the Lord makes allowances for them. This is for carnal Christians who do not make time to read their Bibles adequately. This is for those in whose hearts the Word of God does not abide.

"Study to shew thyself approved unto God, a workman that needeth not to be ashamed, rightly dividing the word of truth." Unless we know the meaning of a passage in its Scriptural setting we are not good students.

We have asked the questions, Do I know the Author? Do I know the meaning? Do I know the application? Do I know the prophetic significance? Now we must ask the question, Do I know the context?

CHAPTER XIII

THE BIBLE—DO I KNOW THE COMPLETE REVELATION?

IT is not enough to know the immediate context of a passage. If we are to be good workmen, we must know the teaching of the whole Bible.

This involves reading the whole Book. It is unfair to say that we cannot understand a book that we have never read. It is impossible to know the message of a book we have never read. Every Christian has read parts of the Bible, but many have never taken time to read the whole Bible. In our devotional reading we may turn again and again to passages that have been a blessing in the past, but when we approach the Bible as a student we must consider the entire book.

There are many ways to read the Bible. Perhaps the most effective is the most elementary—just start with Genesis and keep reading. If more variety is desired, we can read two chapters from the Old Testament and two from the New every day until it is finished. There are many Scripture reading courses that will take us right through the Bible in a given length of time.

It does not matter how we do it, but we must do it, or we are not in a position to call ourselves students of the Word of God. Just as we can arrive at a totally erroneous conclusion by taking a verse out of its context, so we can be misled by taking an isolated truth out of

THE BIBLE

its relative position with what the rest of the Bible reaches about the same truth.

Obscure Passages

This is true to a greater extent with the obscure passages. Usually the difficult verses can be interpreted in the light of the simple verses that deal with the same subject. A clear passage should never be interpreted in the light of an obscure passage. If our rendering of a complicated portion of the Bible contradicts the clear teaching of the rest of the Bible on any issue, we can conclude that we are wrong, and we should begin to search for a meaning that fits into the framework of the rest of Scripture.

Unpardonable Sin

There has always been a certain amount of controversy among Christians about the verses dealing with the unpardonable sin. The same incident is recorded three times in the New Testament and the words of Jesus are being quoted: "All manner of sin and blasphemy shall be forgiven unto men: but the blasphemy against the Holy Ghost shall not be forgiven unto men" (Matt. 12: 31).

If the Lord was talking about individuals in these verses, it would seem that there is some kind of sin a man can commit that is so desperate in the eyes of God that it can never be forgiven. Any person who committed this sin could never be saved. The sin would be unpardonable. It would be the one thing that a man can do that would put him beyond the reach of God's salvation.

The sin that cannot be forgiven has bothered a great many people and they wonder if they may have committed it. Some think it means swearing at or about the Holy Ghost. Others believe it is to attribute the work of the Holy Ghost to Satan, or that these words about the Holy Ghost are simply a way of describing some personal sin that is so evil it cannot be forgiven—perhaps murder or immorality. These are a few of the many explanations.

I am not positively certain as to the real meaning of this passage. It is difficult. Certainly it is obscure. However, we do know the positive teaching of the rest of the Bible about the scope of salvation. If the Bible is clear about who can be saved, then by the process of elimination we can find out who cannot be saved. Obviously, the person who cannot be saved is the one who has committed the unpardonable sin and if these words are referring to individuals at all, this is the man they are talking about—the man who cannot be saved—the man who has committed the unpardonable sin.

The Bible says that anyone who calls upon the Lord can be saved: "Whosoever shall call on the name of the Lord shall be saved" (Acts 2: 21 and Rom. 10: 13).

The Bible says that anyone who will take the water of life can be saved: "Whosoever will, let him take the water of life freely" (Rev. 22: 17).

The Bible says that anyone who believes in Christ can be saved: "For God so loved the world, that he gave his only begotten Son, that whosoever believeth

THE BIBLE

in him should not perish, but have everlasting life" (John 3: 16).

The Bible says that anyone who comes to Christ can be saved: "Him that cometh to me I will in no wise cast out" (John 6: 37). "Come unto me, all ye that labour and are heavy laden, and I will give you rest" (Matt. 11: 28).

The Bible says that anyone who receives Christ can be saved: "As many as received him, to them gave he power to become the sons of God, even to them that believe on his name" (John 1: 12).

These verses are just illustrative of scores of similar passages throughout the whole Bible. They state clearly that anyone who will call, take, believe, come, or receive can be saved. There are no exceptions made in any of these instances. Therefore, we may logically conclude that the only person who cannot be saved is the one who will not call, take, believe, come, or receive. Any single verse that states otherwise would be contradicting the teaching of the rest of the Bible.

Regardless of the terms that Jesus uses, if He intends His words to apply in our age rather than the age of law and if He is speaking about individuals rather than a nation, then the blasphemy against the Holy Ghost would have to be refusal on the part of man to accept Christ as Saviour.

If we were to limit our study to these few verses apart from the rest of the Bible on the same subject, we would be utterly confused and might come to the wrong conclusion—one that contradicts the rest of the Bible. By a knowledge of the whole book we avoid the danger of basing an opinion upon an obscure and difficult passage.

Study the whole Bible. It will throw light upon the difficult parts, and in the process of reading, it will cleanse and direct our lives. "The entrance of thy words giveth light; it giveth understanding unto the simple" (Ps. 119: 130).

"Study to shew thyself approved unto God, a workman that needeth not to be ashamed, rightly dividing the word of truth". We cannot divide the Word properly unless we know the complete revelation.

We have asked the questions, Do I know the Author? Do I know the Meaning? Do I know the Application? Do I know the Prophetic Significance? Do I know the Context? Now we should ask ourselves, Do I know the Complete Revelation?

CHAPTER XIV

THE BIBLE—DO I KNOW AN INFERENCE FROM A FACT?

DO I know the difference between a human assumption or inference and a direct scriptural statement? There is a vast segment of Scripture about which nobody needs to argue. We often refer to these truths as the Fundamentals. The great basic principles of the Bible are always set forth, not once, but many times in the form of direct statements of fact.

As opposed to the facts of Scripture, there is a myriad of interesting details that God has not chosen to fully amplify, but from which we delight to draw conclusions or make assumptions. Many of the divisions in the Christian Church spring from nothing more than these inferences.

The dictionary defines the word *assumption* as "the act of taking for granted". The word *inference* is defined as "arriving at a conclusion on the basis of evidence". It is important that we remember that either of these may be right or wrong. An assumption is often a very well founded guess and an inference may seem to be a logical conclusion. The first is on rather shaky ground at best and the second is determined by the accuracy of our reasoning powers which are never infallible.

The Wet Man

If the door of my office were to open suddenly and a man burst in, soaked to the skin and dripping water from head to toe, I would probably jump to the conclusion that it was raining very heavily. In such an instance, nine times out of ten my inference would be correct. However, it could be entirely wrong. Although everything in the picture would seem to point toward the conclusion that it is raining, this man might have got wet in some other manner. Perhaps he slipped and fell into a puddle or some practical joker may have dumped a barrel of water on him. These are improbable conclusions but they are possible. The wet man points toward rain but he does not prove rain.

With this start we might argue for months about whether it was raining but without further evidence our most carefully phrased conclusions would have to remain in the category of an inference or human assumption.

The Power of the Blood

Suppose someone asks; "Is the blood an essential part of Christian forgiveness?" How would a good Bible student answer such a question?

He might go back in the Old Testament to the story of Cain and Abel. He would describe the characters of these two men in minute detail. Then he would point out the difference in their sacrifices; When Cain came to God he brought the work of his hands; Abel brought an animal and shed its blood; Cain was

THE BIBLE

condemned, Abel was forgiven. Therefore, the shedding of blood is essential if man is to be forgiven for his sins.

This is a good Bible story and the inference that has been made is apparently quite sensible. However, if this was the only Scripture we had about the forgiveness of sin as it relates to the shedding of blood, we could not be dogmatic about it. The fact that it was true once does not of necessity mean that it would be true in every case. In the language of the logician this is an example of generalizing from a particular case and, of course, it is not good logic.

The reason that I can use this Old Testament record to illustrate the place of blood in the forgiveness of sins is that the principle is stated elsewhere. Very clearly in the Bible, without any kind of analogy or inference or human assumption, God states that this is a fact. "Almost all things are by the law purged with blood; and without shedding of blood is no remission" (Hebrews 9: 22).

My assumption from this Old Testament story becomes valid only if it is based on a direct Scriptural statement.

Works For Salvation

Here is another question, "Can a man be saved by works?" How should the Bible student deal with this?

He could start with the story of the thief on the cross and point out the fact that he was saved without works. Here is a case where a great sinner was obviously saved but had no opportunity to earn his own salvation. Therefore, it is obvious that man cannot be saved by works. Once again we have used a particular instance from which to make a general statement: the thief on the cross was saved without works; therefore, anyone can be saved without works.

Even the casual reader of the Bible knows that works cannot save but if we had no other evidence apart from the story of the thief on the cross, this would not be a valid assumption. It becomes valid only when we can turn to other bold statements in the Word of God where no inference of any kind is necessary and find that this truth is stated; "For by grace are ye saved through faith; and that not of yourself; it is the gift of God; not of works lest any man should boast" (Ephesians 2: 8-9).

The Devil

I preach a sermon on Satan in which the major passages of Scripture I use do not at any point mention his name—Ezekiel 28 and Isaiah 14. I believe that the King of Tyre mentioned by Ezekiel can be none other than the devil, and that Lucifer, whose fall is described vividly by Isaiah, is also his satanic majesty.

There are a number of reasons why I believe both these passages refer to Satan and describe his fall. However, I am quite conscious of the fact that the majority of Old Testament commentators do not agree with this interpretation. The historical commentators believe that the description in Ezekiel is a hyperbolic account of the actual King of Tyre, or that it is his impression of himself set forth in the language of poetic exaggeration. Many of the premillennial prophetic commentators think that Lucifer is nothing more than an actual star that fell.

If I were to base my doctrine of the devil on these two passages by themselves, I would be forced into many assumptions or inferences and for that reason I could not be dogmatic about them. If I am able to find other passages of Scripture that pinpoint basic facts in Satan's creation and career in straight-forward statements, then, of course, these Old Testament stories became outstanding illustrations of this career and can quite reasonably be taken as actual accounts of the fall of the devil.

Whether the Bible student wishes to interpret the stories of the King of Tyre and Lucifer as stories of the fall of Satan or not, his doctrine of the devil should be the same as the man who accepts these accounts. There is a vast field of Scriptural references about the devil in the form of unquestionable statements which parallel the descriptions of the King of Tyre and Lucifer. It is quite easy to prove that Satan was an angel, that he was the leader of a large band of angels, that he lived where angels lived, that he sinned through pride and rebellion against the truth of God, that he was judged by the death of Christ on the cross, and that his judgment is to be finally executed in a series of events during which he is cast out of Heaven into the lake of fire.

We can be absolutely dogmatic about the part blood has in the forgiveness of sin, the utter inefficacy of works as a means of salvation, and the fact of the devil's fall.

There are stories, analogies, and types all through the Bible that can be used to illustrate and amplify each of these truths but their validity does not rest upon the inferences or assumptions drawn from these illustrations. They are based upon the solid, direct facts of Scripture.

It is intensely interesting and extremely profitable to investigate and discuss many ideas that are the result of our human assumptions or inferences, and each individual has every right to be firmly convicted of the results of his own Biblical investigation. However, it is a tragedy when a Christian will allow such differences, based only upon human reasoning, to be a point upon which he divides himself from other Christians. It is even more tragic when a large denomination is created upon some doctrine that is a result of a good human assumption or an apparently sensible inference, rather than a solid fact that is set forth boldly and without question in the Bible.

I believe my own assumptions with all my heart, but I cannot object dogmatically if someone disagrees with me. On the other hand, if a person who professes to believe the Bible preaches a doctrine that is clearly contradicted by the hard facts of Scripture, then I must disagree with that man unequivocally.

We have asked the questions, Do I know the Author? Do I know the meaning? Do I know the application? Do I know the prophetic significance? Do I know the context? Do I know the complete revelation? Now we should ask ourselves the question, Do I know the difference between a human assumption or inference and a direct Scriptural statement?

CHAPTER XV

THE BIBLE—DO I KNOW WHO IS SPEAKING?

THERE are only three persons who speak in the Bible—God, the devil, and man. No study of a passage can ever be complete unless we know who is talking.

God Speaks

God talks in three ways. Sometimes he speaks directly. The Old Testament in particular is saturated with the voice of God Himself recorded by a human agent. On almost every page we find the words, "thus saith the Lord . . ." or, "the Lord spake unto. . .".

Very often God speaks through the angels. It was an angel that spoke to the prophet Balaam in the twenty-second chapter of Numbers. In the first part of the same chapter God chose to speak directly, but in the last section He sent His message through an angel. The birth of John the Baptist was announced to his father by an angel. Gabriel was sent to Nazareth to announce the birth of the Messiah to the virgin Mary. In each case God spoke but used an angel as His messenger.

A great deal of the New Testament is filled with the voice of God speaking through the Lord Jesus Christ. When we hear the words of Jesus we hear the voice of God because Jesus is God.

As soon as we have identified the fact that God is speaking, either directly, through the angels, or in the person of His Son, we know that what we read is absolutely reliable. It is the truth.

The Devil Speaks

The second person who speaks in the Bible is the devil. What the devil says is always recorded accurately in the Word of God. We need have no doubt that he actually said these things. However, the content of his words is often quite inaccurate. In the eighth chapter of John, Jesus warns the people: "There is no truth in him. When he speaketh a lie, he speaketh of his own: for he is a liar, and the father of it."

In the dawn of human history his satanic majesty uncoiled before the first mother and discharged his diabolical venom. "Ye shall not surely die: For God doth know that in the day ye eat thereof, then your eyes shall be opened, and ye shall be as gods, knowing good and evil."

It is true that this is exactly what the devil said to Eve but what he said is not true. He promised that they would not die if they followed his advice, but everybody knows that they did die. As a matter of fact, it was their act of transgression against God that caused them to die, and from that day to this everyone has been subject to death.

The Bible is authentic in its quotations of the devil's words but his words may be completely unauthentic.

THE BIBLE

Man Speaks

The final person who speaks in the Bible is man, and although his words are always accurately recorded, what he says may be either true or false.

It is true that Job's wife urged him to "curse God and die", but this can scarcely be taken as good advice. These are the words of a human being capable of being fraught with deep insight and profound thought but also prone to be riddled with incomplete conclusions, prevarications, and inexperience. The disciples professed without exception that they would die before they would deny their Lord and the twenty-sixth chapter of Matthew is faithful in recording exactly what they said: "Peter said unto him, Though I should die with thee, yet will I not deny thee. Likewise also said all the disciples."

This is a reliable record of the historical facts. This is what the disciples said, but you have only to read a few more verses to discover that under the pressure of the enemy's fire, one by one they forsook Jesus until only one man was left in the palace of the high priest. Peter was out on the porch openly denying Christ, and as far as we know, the others were not even there.

Who Said So?

Someone opens the door of my office and announces himself with these words, "Your wife has inherited a million dollars!"

What would be my immediate reaction? Would I begin to make elaborate plans for the future? Would I make arrangements to pay off the mortgage on my house? Or would I go downtown and begin to spend her money? I would do none of these things. I would turn to the man who made this bombastic statement and ask one simple question, "Who says so?" My actions would be determined entirely by the source of his information. There are certain people whom I would trust. There are others whom I consider unreliable, and a few who are practical jokers.

Early in our study of any passage of Scripture it is vitally important that we find out who is talking. The words of God are one hundred per cent reliable whether they come directly, through the angels, or through Jesus Christ. The words of man may be either true or false.

We have asked the questions: Do I know the Author? Do I know the meaning? Do I know the application? Do I know the prophetic significance? Do I know the context? Do I know the complete revelation? Do I know the difference between an inference and a fact? Now we need to ask the question: Do I know who is speaking?

CHAPTER XVI

THE BIBLE—DO I KNOW TO WHOM IT IS SPEAKING?

THERE are two Dr. Smiths in The Peoples Church. Dr. Oswald J. Smith has an office on the second floor and my office is on the main floor. Very often when people telephone they simply ask for Dr. Smith, and it is very important that our receptionist finds out which one they want and then presses the button that will connect the caller with the right office. If she did not properly divide the calls, a great deal of confusion would result.

In his second letter to Timothy the Apostle Paul urges him to study the Bible carefully so that he will learn to apply it to the right people. "Study to shew thyself approved unto God, a workman that needeth not to be ashamed, rightly dividing the word of truth."

A Tent-Maker

The picture in Paul's mind might well have been that of a tent-maker who would cut pieces of canvas in certain shapes to fit particular areas of the tent he was about to make. He would place those which went on the fronts in one pile and those for the backs in another, and so on. If he did not rightly divide the pieces he might put a section that belonged on the side in the area of the floor and there would be no end of difficulty simply because it was not put in its proper place.

This is what is involved in rightly dividing the Bible. It must be cut straight and applied to the people to whom it was spoken. There are four kinds of people addressed in the Bible:

Everybody

Much of it is for everybody. When the Psalmist says, "Blessed is the man that walketh not in the counsel of the ungodly", he is speaking to the world. This is a principle that applies in any age and under any conditions. When Jesus said, "Come unto me, all ye that labour and are heavy laden, and I will give you rest", He was thinking in terms of the entire world. There is no one who is barred from this universal invitation.

Particular Individuals

Some areas of the Bible speak to particular people in the world. Noah was told to build an ark. Jonah was commanded to preach in Nineveh. God told Joshua to march around the city of Jericho. Jesus sent the seventy disciples out to preach the Gospel and told them to take no purse with them. Jesus called twelve disciples and it is quite obvious that they not only had a purse but they had a man whose office it was to carry it.

It is important when we read such passages that we realize that these are commands to particular people in the world. God never told anybody else to build an

THE BIBLE

ark or preach in Nineveh or capture a city by marching around it or go out without a purse. These are not instructions to people in general or even to God's own people. These apply to particular men at a specific time in world history to meet a definite need.

This does not mean that these stories have no relation to us and therefore are a waste of valuable time. The great principle behind all of these is that we should obey God despite the fact that we may not understand the implications of His commands or see the final outcome. It is relatively unimportant that Noah built the ark; it is vitally important that he obeyed God. As far as we are concerned the preaching of Jonah in the city of Nineveh is inconsequential; the fact that Jonah eventually obeyed God has tremendous implications for us. The story of the fall of Jericho under the command of Joshua is not a lesson in military strategy; it is an outstanding example of unwavering faith in God.

We could get into serious trouble and create many problems for other people if we attempted to do the work of God without some kind of financial support; the big thing about the story of the seventy disciples is that they took Jesus at His word and went forth on that particular occasion without a purse.

The Jewish People

Occasionally the Bible is addressed specifically to the Jews. In the twenty-third chapter of Matthew Jesus is lamenting over the spiritual condition of the Jewish Nation: "O Jerusalem, Jerusalem, thou that killest the prophets, and stoneth them which are sent unto thee, how often would I have gathered thy children together, even as a hen gathereth her chickens under her wings, and ye would not!"

This passage is not for the world nor is it for any particular person. It is addressed directly to the Jew, and there are many other passages that are in the same category.

The Church

Finally, there are sections of the Bible that are devoted entirely to the Christian.

The Book of Romans says, "I beseech you therefore, brethren, by the mercies of God, that ye present your bodies a living sacrifice, holy, acceptable unto God, which is your reasonable service".

This exhortation has nothing to do with the world at large nor has it anything to do with any particular person in the world, and it certainly has no direct application to the Jewish nation. It is addressed to the group called "brethren" which in the New Testament nearly always refers to men and women who have trusted Jesus Christ as their Saviour and have become members of the living Church. To these people the Bible says, "present your bodies".

In the thirteenth chapter of his first letter to the Corinthian church, the Apostle Paul makes it very clear that it is utterly useless for anyone else to do this. As a matter of fact, it is a sheer waste of time. "Though I give my body to be burned, and have not charity, it profiteth me nothing."

The Apostle Paul urges the Christian to avoid conformity with the world. "Be not conformed to this

THE BIBLE

world: but be ye transformed by the renewing of your mind."

Nowhere does the Bible ask the Godless man to be different from the world. He is not expected to do so and indeed it is impossible for him. He is of the world and until he has been born again he will always be worldly. He will act in conformity with the society in which he lives. However, the Christian, and only the Christian, is expected to follow the injunction of the Book of Romans and press upstream against the tide of worldly affairs.

The Word of God may become an entirely different book after you have learned to "rightly divide" it. All of it should be a source of blessing or conviction to everyone who reads it. I cannot close any part of it and say, this is not for me, therefore I will ignore it. By doing so I may miss some of the greatest blessings that come from inspiration and analogy and application, but in the final interpretation of any passage it is essential that I know who is being addressed.

Before leaving this section it should be noted that no man can be an infallible judge of the division of every passage. Most of the time the context makes it quite obvious to which of the four classes a given passage is directed. However, there are other places where it is not clear and indeed may apply to more than one of the groups. For instance, the extreme dispensationalist insists that the twenty-fourth chapter of Matthew refers only to Israel and has no reference to the Church at all. However most Bible scholars have always felt that these verses have a duel application—to Israel and also to the Church.

When we ask the question, To Whom Is It Speaking? we should remember that in some cases we do not know for sure, but that in many instances it is obvious, and makes a difference in our interpretation.

We have asked the questions, Do I Know the Author? Do I Know the Meaning? Do I Know the Application? Do I Know the Prophetic Significance? Do I Know the Context? Do I Know the Complete Revelation? Do I Know the Difference Between an Inference and a Direct Statement? and Do I Know Who is Speaking? Now we should ask the question, Do I Know to Whom It is Speaking?

CHAPTER XVII

THE BIBLE—DO I KNOW THE EXPERIENCE OF OBEDIENCE?

IT comes as rather a shock to the medical student when he graduates from a six or eight-year course in a university to discover that his education really begins after his school days are over.

It is a frustrating experience for the young minister to enter his first charge with a minimum of seven years of college and seminary behind him only to learn that he has never been taught most of the things he needs to know.

It is rather bewildering for the man who has just passed his bar examinations to begin work as a junior member of some firm to find that most of the cases with which he is asked to deal are exceptions to the rules rather than examples.

These and many others are illustrations of one of the unpleasant phenomena of life—the disparity between theory and practice. The farmer, the professional man, the tradesman, the business girl, and even the mother, do not compete long in the rugged area of real life before they are faced with this very difficult transitional period between the knowledge that has been stored in their minds and the ability they need in the functional application of it.

Knowledge and Practice

The field of Bible Study is no exception to the rule. It is one thing to know the Bible. It is quite another to put it into practice. Sometimes the people who can explain the Bible the best seem to live it the worst. Hebrew and Greek may be as familiar to some students as their native tongue, but ethics, morality, and righteousness are foreign languages to them. This is what concerned the Apostle James when he wrote these words: "But be ye doers of the word, and not hearers only, deceiving your own selves.

"For if any be a hearer of the word, and not a doer, he is like unto a man beholding his natural face in a glass:

"For he beholdeth himself, and goeth his way, and straightway forgetteth what manner of man he was.

"But whoso looketh into the perfect law of liberty, and continueth therein, he being not a forgetful hearer, but a doer of the work, this man shall be blessed in his deed" (James 1: 22-25).

God's Looking Glass

James is using a rather humorous illustration with which all of us are familiar in the scope of our own experience. I look into the mirror and it tells me unmistakably that my face is dirty or my hair is untidy or my tie is not straight. Then something else demands my attention or some other thought floods my mind and I turn away without doing what the mirror has suggested. When I go outside in this condition, I become the laughing stock of those who

THE BIBLE

see me, and this will continue throughout the day until I go back inside and do what the mirror says.

The Word of God is not only an accurate account of religious history, a series of exciting stories about men and women who lived many hundreds of years ago, or a collection of the finest principles of life that have ever been put together in one volume. The Bible is a Divine looking-glass. From its shiny pages we see reflected the images of ourselves and our personal needs.

If the story of King Saul does not throw a light on some of the problems of my own life, then I have read it in vain. If the appalling account of the scarlet sin of David and Bathsheba does not convey a message to my own heart, then I have wasted the time it took to read it. If I can read the magnificent ethics of the Sermon on the Mount without becoming conscious of the unethical smudges on my own character, I have missed the point. If I read the lucid salvation passages of the Gospel of John without being aware of my own need of forgiveness and God's provision for my salvation, I am of all men most unfortunate.

In each of these cases, I would be like the man envisioned by the Apostle who has looked into the mirror and has seen what manner of man he was, but has refused to take heed.

The Purpose of the Bible

The study of the Bible is a fascinating endeavour but it is never an end in itself. The accumulation of prophetic promises is intriguing in a marked degree, but that is not the purpose of the Bible. A beautiful essay on the literary architecture of the Book would be an illuminating pursuit, but it might be quite in vain. A vast storehouse of memorized Bible passages could be as useless as a casket of pearls in a pig pen.

First and last, the Word of God must speak personally to the man who reads it and studies it, and he must respond to its exhortations, obey its commands, and seek to live in accordance with its principles.

We have asked the questions Do I Know the Author? Do I Know the Meaning? Do I Know the Application? Do I Know the Prophetic Significance? Do I Know the Context? Do I Know the Complete Revelation? Do I Know the Difference Between an Inference and a Direct Statement? Do I Know Who is Speaking? Do I Know to Whom It is Speaking? Finally, we must ask the question, Do I Know the Experience of Obedience to the Commands of the Bible?